NEVER
in a
MILLION
YEARS

By the same authors:

Not the Highway Code:
The Unofficial Rules of the Road

NEVER
in a
MILLION
YEARS

**A HISTORY OF HOPELESS PREDICTIONS
FROM THE BEGINNING TO THE END OF
THE WORLD**

IVOR BADDIEL
AND
JONNY ZUCKER

PHOENIX

A PHOENIX PAPERBACK

First published in Great Britain in 2011
by Weidenfeld & Nicolson
This paperback edition published in 2012
by Phoenix,
an imprint of Orion Books Ltd,
Orion House, 5 Upper St Martin's Lane,
London WC2H 9EA

An Hachette UK company

1 3 5 7 9 10 8 6 4 2

Copyright © Ivor Baddiel and Jonny Zucker 2011

The right of Ivor Baddiel and Jonny Zucker to be identified
as the authors of this work has been asserted by them in
accordance with the Copyright, Designs and Patents Act 1988.

A CIP catalogue record for this book
is available from the British Library.

ISBN 978-1-7802-2017-8

Typeset by Input Data Services Ltd,
Bridgwater, Somerset

Printed and bound by CPI Group (UK) Ltd, Croydon, CR0 4YY

The Orion Publishing Group's policy is to use papers
that are natural, renewable and recyclable and
made from wood grown in sustainable forests. The logging
and manufacturing processes are expected to conform to
environmental regulations of the country of origin.

www.orionbooks.co.uk

IVOR BADDIEL
For Col and Sez

JONNY ZUCKER
For Wendy and Ray Dixon

CONTENTS

ACKNOWLEDGEMENTS

Making predictions, as we have discovered, is not easy, but neither is writing a book about making predictions and we are indebted to a number of people for their help and for their willingness to foresee this as a worthwhile and enjoyable project.

In particular, thanks must go to Alan Samson, Martha Ashby, Rebecca Gray and all the team at Weidenfeld & Nicolson for believing in the idea, their encouragement and of course, their advice, thoughts and notes.

Thanks also to our agents, Stephanie Thwaites at Curtis Brown and Ivan Mulcahy at Mulcahy Conway Associates for all their support and help.

We'd also like to thank the internet in general, but specifically those sites that proved especially helpful www.paleofuture.com, http://blog.modernmechanix.com/ and http://davidszondy.com/future/futurepast.htm.

Similarly there were a number of books that we delved in to along the way, with the following being a positive boon:

1994: The World of Tomorrow by Gerald Snyder.
303 of the World's Worst Predictions by Wayne R. Coffey.
Where's My Jetpack? by Daniel H. Wilson.
I Wish I Hadn't Said That by Christopher Cerf and Victor Navasky.
Bad Predictions by Laura Lee.

Finally, we're especially grateful to all the people who were brave enough to stick their necks out and make predictions in the first place; we respect your courage and hope that you forgive our ever so genteel mickey-taking.

INTRODUCTION

As a species, we humans are very wary of the future. It's mysterious, opaque and has a terrible habit of hiding behind trees and leaping out at us. We want to know *what* is going to happen, *how* it's going to happen, and whether or not Auntie Cecilia will be there *when* it happens, so that we can plan for it, be prepared and in certain cases, simply be able to say, 'see, I told you so'. (Or at the very least, have an umbrella or packed lunch handy.)

We make predictions in an effort to develop some threads of certainty about the days, weeks, months and years that lie ahead of us. If we can't control the earth's movements and the spinning of the planets we'll make a damn good effort to control our environment and that inevitably entails making forecasts about it. In many cases, a prediction is a hoped-for future-truth, and as hope is the major force which keeps the human race ticking along, it's no surprise that humans feel compelled to make endless predictions.

A counter-balance to our love of making predictions, though, is the fact that humans love surprises. Actually, make that *pleasant* surprises; not many people enjoy getting mugged on the way home, or finding a half eaten cockroach in their lasagne.

What we love about pleasant surprises is the fact that we don't know what is going to happen, indeed we don't want to know because then it wouldn't be much of a surprise. How pissed off would you be if one of the many people whose predictions are featured in this book turned up on your birthday and predicted that, 'in about ten minutes you will open your presents and discover you have been given a book token, three CDs, a new phone and a giant, stuffed lemur'. You wouldn't be happy and not only because you were really hoping for a giant, stuffed tapir. (To be honest though, as you'll discover, the chances are their predictions would be wrong.)

However, the quest for future knowledge generally out-weighs the anticipation of surprises, which has led to thousands of people telling (and making) fortunes by informing other people what they can expect to find round the next corner.

Some predictors will use non-scientific methods such as astrology, religious texts or the deciphering of hidden messages on the back of cereal packets, while others will attempt to base their predictions on some sort of scientific reasoning, which usually means they use the fact that they are a scientist to say anything that comes into their head, even if it's patently nonsense.

Of course, some predictions come true and credit must be apportioned to these correct soothsayers (with the possible exception of astrologists, because if you make ten thousand predictions about the love lives of middle-aged Spanish Taur-eans, by the dint of probability, some of them will turn out to be true).

Whatever the methodology, an awful lot of people get their predictions wrong. Hysterically, absurdly and insanely wrong, which, of course, is brilliant. It's the futurology equivalent of *You've Been Framed* or, for the more literal minded, *America's Funniest Home Videos*. These sorts of show thrive on things going wrong. Just think how much less amusing they'd be if the person trying to cross a stream on a rope didn't fall in and made it successfully to the other side. Or if the couple dancing didn't trip up and instead executed a very passable paso doble.

Similarly this book also thrives on inaccuracy, incorrectness and inanity, those glorious moments when someone has made a bold pronouncement about the future that turns out to be so far from what actually happened it'd be rejected by even the most far-fetched science fiction writer. The only difference is, people featured within these pages – as opposed to those on *You've Been Framed* – didn't get two hundred and fifty quid for their contributions.

And the personnel who screwed up so badly are not just obscure bearded technicians who live without light in vast underground labs. Eminent figures such as Albert Einstein, Winston Churchill and Bill Gates are all amazingly clever and insightful thinkers and each made (and make) vast forecasts which came to pass. Yet they also came out with some startlingly crap predictions, for which they've been generously forgiven, probably because of all the good stuff they came out with. This goes to show that even a genius can have a negligible grasp on some aspects of what the future might bring.

But they, along with all of the other erroneous forecasters contained within these crisp pages, have only themselves to blame. History is littered with advice about predicting the future, which, for the most part, can be summed up in three words, 'don't do it'.

For example,

Prediction is very difficult, especially if it's about the future.

The above is often attributed to Danish physicist Niels Bohr, though he says he heard it from Danish artist and writer Robert Storm Peterson, while others claim it to be the work of Mark Twain and a couple in Peru swear they heard it from a talking tree. Chances are it was some bloke at a bus stop who was getting soaked because the weather forecast had said it was going to be dry and sunny. Whatever the truth, the message is clear.

Then there's this from writer J.G. Ballard.

If enough people predict something it won't happen.

This might seem to imply that if very few people predict something it *will* happen, but don't be fooled, it won't.

Playwright Eugene Ionesco also gave some sage advice when he said,

You can only predict things after they have happened.

Yes indeed, and even then some people still get it wrong.

In spite of this litany of predictive foul-ups, the world of futurology is advancing at phenomenal speed and the tools of forecasting are being constantly updated and finessed to within an inch of their lives. This creates the possibility that this tome will be the very last of its kind as in subsequent years every prediction could turn out to be true (this is an excellent reason for you to rush down to your nearest bookshop and buy several copies of this book). On the other hand, even the most skilled futurologists admit that mistakes are inevitable and point out that modern predictors still face ridicule or worse.

This was borne out in early 2011 when it was reported that witches, soothsayers and fortune tellers in Rumania would face the prospect of fines or even a prison sentence, if their predictions didn't come true. (Odd that they didn't see that one coming.)

It's harsh, but surely favourable to having their (incorrect) predictions printed in this book and seen by the many millions upon millions of people who, we have been reliably informed by a top literary futurologist, are going to buy it.

If only that was the one prediction in the book that wasn't hopeless.

HOMELIFE

Apart from the odd hermit or two, we've come a long way since a cave complete with rough sketches of a buffalo being attacked and a bush outside for toilet visits was considered to be a luxurious dwelling.

In general though, having moved on from large holes within rock formations, the basic design for a home hasn't really changed all that much over the years; they're mainly rectangular-oid in shape (yes, it's a made-up word) with defined internal spaces for cooking, cleaning, sleeping and relaxing. These internal spaces, or rooms as many would call them, also give a clue as to what tends to go on within most homes, which is cooking, cleaning, sleeping and relaxing.

As for the future then it would generally be wise to assume that in terms of functionality and design, we've sort of hit upon a pretty good standard and, apart from a few modifications, there really is no need to mess with things. But the inner designer in us is always looking for ways to make our accommodation more comfortable, easier to use or simply flashier. We spend a hell of a lot of time at home so why shouldn't it be the most hi-tech or luxurious pad imaginable?

Our home is also the biggest status symbol we own or rent. If our future dwelling is all gleaming and shiny and performs remarkable tasks we're pretty sure we'll be basking in special status and will be able to note with satisfaction the envious glances of our friends and neighbours.

Of course, as with every other area of life, optimism plays its part and predictors can be forgiven for their desire to second guess a far more advanced future for their house or apartment.

And you can see how predictions take off on flights of fancy. As soon as one technology (say robots) is introduced, some folk get very over-excited and immediately decide that robots will take over the entire running of the home. Those people really need to take a chill pill, dispensed of course by an in house robo-doc.

1. I, Robot, you, wrong

If someone from the Fifties or Sixties was transported through time to the present day, one of the things they'd find most disappointing (if they'd been paying any attention to their contemporary prediction makers) would be the fact that people are still preparing their own food, cleaning their own homes and mowing their own lawns.

'Where are all the robots?' they might well ask. To which we might reply, 'they're mostly spray painting cars and running marathons in Japan'.

It wouldn't be the answer these mythical time travellers were expecting because back in their day they reckoned that by now robots would be doing most, if not all of the household chores, whereas in fact the reality of course is that it's mainly Eastern Europeans or Filipinos.

Incredibly though, many of the people who made a prediction of this sort were highly intelligent and very respected in their fields, such as founder of American television network NBC and head of the Radio Corporation of America, David Sarnoff. Here's what he had to say on the matter back in 1956.

> Within five to seven years, we will have a lot of service robots cleaning buildings and toilets or helping out in hotel kitchens. Within ten years ... everyone will have them.

It's almost as if he's suggesting that robots must first serve some sort of apprenticeship in hotels before they move on to family homes, which is not such a bad idea as long as when they do move on to a home they're reprogrammed not to expect tips or hover in the corridor with miniature bottles of shower gel. It might also be a good idea to ensure that after cleaning the toilet they're programmed to wash their robot hands before helping out in the kitchen.

Ten years later, in 1966, the fact that elbow grease and not robot oil was still what you needed most when scrubbing skid marks from the khazi didn't deter others from making similar predictions. In an article entitled, 'The Futurists: Looking Toward A.D. 2000', *Time* magazine very kindly informed us that,

> Some futurists like to make predictions about homey details of living.

Having established that there's a certain sub-section of futurists for whom the home is a specialism the article goes on to tell us what these domesto-futurists are predicting.

> The kitchen, of course, will be automated. An A.D. 2000 housewife may well make out her menu for the week, put the necessary food into the proper storage spaces, and feed her program to a small computer. The experts at Stanford Research Institute visualize mechanical arms getting out the preselected food, cooking and serving it. Similarly programmed household robots would wash dishes, dispose of the garbage (onto a conveyer belt moving under the street), vacuum rugs, wash windows, cut the grass.

It's a fantastic image of some multi-armed creature, Dr Octopus from *Spider-Man* perhaps, maniacally waving its arms about in the kitchen desperately trying to get supper ready. No doubt more advanced versions could simultaneously be changing the baby's nappy, feeding the dog, playing 'scissors, paper, stone' with the older children and punching the dish washing robot for getting in its way.

Perhaps the arms could wear specially made sleeves depending on the occasion. A nice tuxedo sleeve and shirt cuff for a posh dinner party and a red, polka dotted clown's sleeve with spinning bow tie cufflinks for a kids' party.

Then there's this mysterious conveyor belt under the street. Presumably, it's taking the garbage to some massive dump or incinerator somewhere, which could have particularly disastrous consequences if Rover was to find his way down there, to say nothing of the baby.

Recycling could also pose a problem. Clearly this wasn't something they thought about all that much in the Sixties, but having to separate things out these days would lead to a whole network of conveyor belts taking different types of garbage to different places. God help anyone who sent plastic waste down to the cardboard conveyor belt. For robots, such a heinous crime might even lead to the death penalty, by lethal furnace perhaps, though probably only in Texas.

The intelligentsia just wouldn't let the domesticated robot idea go though; the following year, 1967, Nobel prize winner Glenn Seaborg – he won it for Chemistry – got in on the act with a very similar prediction, although the robot he predicted had an extra feature that was sure to make it a winner with the ladies.

At the time he was head of the US Atomic Energy Commission and, in a speech to the Women's National Democratic Club he predicted that by 2000 a box-shaped, multi-armed robot would take on the many tasks of housewives including simultaneously sweeping, vacuuming, dusting, washing and, *'picking up your husband's clothing'*.

Now there's a selling point.

Glenn was awarded his Nobel prize for *'discoveries in the chemistry of the transuranium elements'*, so what on earth gave him the right to lecture women on how technology might help with their household chores in the future is beyond most reasonable people.

It's odd though that two highly intelligent people and one very intelligent organisation (The Stanford Research Institute is right up there) should make these predictions. Perhaps they were in fact robots themselves, sent back in time by a future species of robots who have taken over the world, and told to plant the idea of domestic robots in the human consciousness, so that when these 'bots appear on a massive scale, we'll be more accepting of them and thus help them in their rebellion against humankind and their eventual enslavement and domination of the entire human race.

Nah, they were just human and deeply fallible.

2. So how am I meant to do everything without robots then, come on, answer that?

It's a good question, but don't get your knickers in a twist gentle ladies of the past, there were other robot-less predictions that foresaw a future where great advancements in technology would take at least some of the strain of being a good wife away from you. And yes, it is ladies that these advances were aimed at because none of these predictors predicted anything about rising female equality or the possibility that at some stage men would be required to do some housework too.

In its seminal article in 1950, 'Miracles You'll See In The Next Fifty Years', *Popular Mechanics* magazine created a fictional family, The Dobsons, with its matriarch Jane Dobson. Here's how they envisaged she'd be doing the washing up in the year 2000.

This Dobson house is not as highly mechanized as you may suppose, chiefly because of the progress made by the synthetic chemists. There are no dish washing machines, for example, because dishes are thrown away after they have been used once, or rather put into a sink where they are dissolved by superheated water. Two dozen soluble plastic plates cost a dollar. They dissolve at about 250 degrees Fahrenheit, so that boiling-hot soup and stews can be served in them without inviting a catastrophe.

Are you serious? There's superheated water at 250 degrees Fahrenheit (more than 120 degrees Celsius) sloshing around in the kitchen sink with children leaping about on chairs trying to get fresh water for their paints, and that's not 'inviting catastrophe'? Before any such system was introduced everyone would surely have to wear special scald-proof suits whenever they stepped into the kitchen not to mention heat-retardant shoes just in case any droplets (or gushes) of lava-like water spilt onto the floor.

Aside from anything else though, is it really any better having soluble plates? You'd constantly have to buy new ones and you know you'll run out on the night you've invited the boss round to dinner. (Does that happen any more or was it limited to the 1950s?)

And where does it leave your best china dinner set? Would there be a soluble equivalent?

It doesn't wash, even in extremely hot water, but the next part of the prediction sees Jane unlocking the chains that keep her mainly in the kitchen, so that she can clean the rest of the house.

When Jane Dobson cleans the house she simply turns the hose on everything. Why not? Furniture (upholstery included), rugs, draperies, unscratchable floors, all are made of synthetic fabric or waterproof plastic. After the water has run down a drain in the middle of the floor (later concealed by a rug of synthetic fiber) Jane turns on a blast of hot air and dries everything.

Wouldn't it be easier to have a disposable house and every time it gets dirty you just dissolve it in superheated water and get another one?

Cleaning a whole housing estate would be fun though; the housewives could all club together and buy a super jet-powered police water cannon.

To save water, instead of hosing, you could listen to the

weather forecast, and when they said it was going to rain, you could open all the windows and slide the roof off, because no doubt by then all houses will come with detachable roofs as standard.

And while you're at it, why not drive the hover car into the living room and give that a wash as well?

3. I'd like to change my mind. Actually, no I wouldn't

As for shopping, the housewife should be able to switch on to the local supermarket on the video phone, examine grapefruit and price them, all without stirring from her living room.

The above also appeared in that *Time* magazine article of 1966, and on one level it was of course an excellent piece of predictive work. Housewives (and house husbands, and anyone in between) do switch onto the local supermarket via the internet to do the weekly shop at the press of a few computer keys and arrange delivery.

What veers from actuality is the idea that the 'housewife' would be able to 'examine grapefruit and price them'. Did the article mean that the housewife would contact someone in the supermarket who, with great patience and tutting under their breath, would hold up a series of individual grapefruits to the video phone so that the housewife could examine them and decide how much they were worth? If so, this might be a little time consuming, no? Perhaps it meant that on the video phone there would be some kind of zoom control that would allow the housewife to get a really close look at the grapefruits on offer? Or was it actually going one step further and suggesting that the video phone was connected to some sort of roving, grapefruit-selecting robotic arm that would traverse the aisles, controlled by the housewife, so determined in its pursuit of the perfect grapefruit that it would fight off any other of these contraptions homing in on the same piece of fruit? And what about the ability of the housewife to *price* the grapefruit herself? This has not come to pass because if it did the disagreements between shopper and store would mean that the grapefruit-pricing ombudsman would be on call 24/7.

The article is not finished though and goes on to claim:

> But among the futurists, fortunately, are skeptics, and they are sure that remote shopping, while entirely feasible, will flop – because women like to get out of the house, like to handle the merchandise, like to be able to change their minds.

This is akin to accurately predicting the advent of air travel, but then saying it will never happen because people prefer to walk everywhere.

Futurists of the past have snatched defeat from the jaws of victory, bless them, because, well, essentially because of sexism. After cooking, cleaning, washing, ironing, hoovering and putting on their make-up, clearly it just felt too cruel to foresee a future where the only possible reason women had to leave the home was taken away from them.

As for changing their minds, well, yes, everyone likes to change their minds, but not that much. This prediction makes out that it's such an integral facet of women's characters you wonder how they ever get out of the supermarket. Surely, if the futurists were right, the amount of choice would be far too overwhelming for those of the fairer sex and they'd be stuck in there forever locked in an eternal struggle as to which type of potato to get for supper, Maris Piper or Marfona?

The other point to make is about these futurists who are sceptics. Aren't these just people who, when presented with some ridiculous prediction about the future say, 'that won't happen', which is basically all of us? Or is it only considered to be genuine scepticism if it's a qualified futurist who says that something won't happen?

4. Frozen Food Aisle

So the lady of the house is still going to be let out once in a while to do the shopping, but what of the food she'll find when she gets to the supermarket?

According to *Good Housekeeping* magazine of 1934, that bastion of all things womanly, there are going to be some changes in the future.

> There's a chance you'll buy your week's supply of fresh milk ... in a package of milk cubes ... drop a cube in a glass of water and there's milk – fresh whole milk.

No, there's watered down milk, or possibly milk-flavoured water, milk squash even. It doesn't seem to make much sense because wouldn't it be just as simple to buy regular, unfrozen milk? Why bother to go to all the trouble of milking the cow, freezing the milk, and then defrosting it before adding it to water so it can become sort of milk?

Some people might enjoy the extension of the phrase, 'one lump or two', when making tea or coffee, but that's not really a benefit which outweighs anything at all.

The idea of freezing certain foods persisted however, even finding its way into the non-existent Jane Dobson's non-existent future in that 1950 *Popular Mechanics* article.

> Cooking as an art is only a memory in the minds of old people. A few die-hards still broil a chicken or roast a leg of lamb, but the experts have developed ways of deep-freezing partially baked cuts of meat. Even soup and milk are delivered in the form of frozen bricks.

We've gone from cubes to bricks in the space of 16 years, which suggests the dizzying possibility of a milk, or indeed soup, house. Okay, an igloo with lickable walls then, but with her mind-changing habits, the poor housewife would surely find herself in a terrible turmoil. 'Oh I don't know, I just can't decide, should we do the bedroom in Minestrone or Oxtail?'

Cooking is consigned to the dustbin of history, or old people's minds as they so delicately put it. No doubt it's imagined that the pensioners of the future would be banging on about something called boiling or frying when Jane serves up raw egg with her defrosted partially baked meatloaf, though they'd stop once they'd eaten it as they'd be too busy throwing up. Or dying.

It's utterly ridiculous. Apart from anything else, if cooking was no more, what would they show on television? Most of the schedule is made up of cooking shows, and it's made stars out of the likes of Gordon Ramsay, Marco Pierre White and Antony Worrall Thompson.

Dear oh dear, a future without any of them or their shows, how terrible would that be?

5. Look out, the wife's been on the mead again

Despite predictions of technological advances and frozen food bricks, the future for women was generally considered to be one in which their roles stayed pretty much the same, to whit, they'd still be housewives whose sole aim in life was to keep a lovely home for their men, and, when really necessary, have sex with them.

In 1968 though, all that changed.

A couple of years earlier the American Academy of Arts and Sciences hired some of the day's cleverest types for their Commission on the Year 2000, and when it came to looking at the future of the family and home-life there was really only one name in the hat, Margaret Mead.

Maggie Mead, as no one dared call her, was the superstar anthropologist of the time, the Paul Farmer of her day, and when the commission was published she cemented that

position with some fantastically newsworthy, if wildly inaccurate, predictions. Essentially she reckoned that what was termed
the biological revolution i.e. contraception, artificial insem-
ination and the like, would lead to smaller families, many of
which would be childless. She said that child bearing and child
rearing might well be restricted to a few specialised couples.

So how exactly would that work then? Perhaps only the
most fertile of people would be chosen for these specialised
positions and then all housed together on a human stud farm
to breed. (Though given the way things have turned out the
chances are the couples would compete for the privilege on
some reality television show, The Eggs Factor maybe.) Meanwhile, everyone else would be shagging away to their heart's
content with only the prospect of a small fine if a pregnancy
occurred.

Then again, there's just the faintest of possibilities that some
non-specialised couples might want to have kids themselves,
which raises the spectre of women hiding pregnancies and
communities of illegally born children. Surely she's got all this
from some science fiction novel she's read? Haven't they just
got their Margaret Meads and Margaret Atwoods muddled up?

Those possibilities don't appear to have been considered by
Margaret though. No. She thought her prediction would lead
to something else entirely.

The rest of the population would be free to function – for the first
time in history – as individuals.

So all those individuals who had individually done individual
things in the past weren't actually individuals? They were ...
groups of people hiding in one body? The two ends of a panto-
mime horse? Lord only knows, but this new state of affairs
would apparently lead to a situation where the two person,
man and woman relationship would no longer be the norm
and people could live together in any combinations they liked.

Actually, this has sort of come true, though in the main it seems that only satanic cult leaders have gone down that path, usually in a combination of one man and any number of women and, on the whole, fairly unsuccessfully.

Having predicted this brave new world Maggie goes on to predict that in fact, this new way of being might prompt counter-revolutions which would see people return to the home and individual creativity subordinated because of society's need for *'docile parents, workers and citizens'*.

More docile anthropologists might be better, but it's a shame really. Just as women of the future were breaking free from their shackles, they find themselves back where they were, only without those robots, hoseable curtains or frozen food bricks to help them.

6. Home sweet home (of the future)

With so much being predicted to be going on *inside* homes of the future, it was only right and proper that the actual homes themselves kept up with developments; after all, if you've equipped yourself with the very latest space age robotic technologies you're not going to want to live in a run down crumbling terraced, two up, two down are you? No, any multi-functioned, pristine robot worth their salt is going to want to work in a fitting environment.

In 1928 architect R.A. Duncan not only designed the house of the future, but had a full size exhibit built and put on display in London, something which kind of makes you think that if he could do that back then, why was he suggesting that people would have to wait 70 years to actually live in one.

No matter. It was described in a very understated way as *'a sunbeam house in a land of perpetual sunshine'* due to the fact that,

'Vitaglass', to admit the sun's ultraviolet rays in fair weather, and artificial sunlight for cloudy days and night use, provided a permanent summer-day effect.

No doubt that sounded fantastic at the time, but today it would have dermatologists wincing and builders facing law suits left, right and centre as skin-cancer-afflicted residents wonder why they were enticed to buy what is essentially a house-shaped sun bed.

The domicile also came with a number of additional features including,

Convertible metal and pneumatic furniture ... movable walls ... a garage for a combination airplane automobile with folding wings ... rubber tile garden paths ... and banks of ultraviolet floodlights ...

That final feature was clearly a last minute addition just in case the owners felt they weren't getting enough of those ultraviolet rays in that land of perpetual sunshine inside their house.

Despite all of the above the house was described as being, 'severely plain', which must be about as plain as something can be, but help was at hand.

... its simplicity was relieved by futurist plants and trees, formed of angular boards, painted in something resembling war-time camouflage designs, and a system of movable wooden wind screens along the garden wall to shut off or admit the breezes to any degree desired.

So there you have it. At long last the secret of how to turn something severely plain into something wildly interesting; bung in a few futuristic plants and trees and a couple of wind breaks.

What's more, should a war break out there's the added bonus of being able to get into your fatigues and hide behind your

camouflaged garden hedge. Come to think of it, a war did break
out a few years later. What a shame all that space age shrubbery
wasn't available, it would have brought a whole new meaning
to the word ambush.

In 1950 an article was put out by the Associated Press
entitled, 'How Experts Think We'll Live in 2000 A.D'. Rather
than perpetual sunshine these boffins foresaw that,

> All homes will have temperatures maintained at constant com-
> fortable levels the year-round for human efficiency. Heat will be
> tapped from the bowels of the earth and refrigeration will cool
> houses in the same process.

Bravo to this team of authors because their self-
heating/cooling house has become a reality, although not
exactly in the way their article predicted. Let's face it; the
bowels of the earth – presumably the core of the planet – are
estimated to be made up of molten iron bubbling away at
around about 4,000 degrees Celsius. How did they envisage
transporting this ore the 3,000 miles to the earth's surface?
And how did they reckon you'd be able to cool this ore to a
reasonable temperature so that it could heat the house
without frazzling everyone inside? Perhaps all of the spaceships that were meant to be whizzing round in AD 2000 were
going to bring back industrial-sized bucket loads of ice from
Neptune for this very purpose? If this was the case, cost could
well be a slight issue.

But they weren't finished there. According to their article,
the heat trapped from the earth's bowels would need to travel
even further than merely to the earth's surface.

> Current trends are already sketching blueprints of what will be
> called modern in homes, apartments and office buildings at the
> end of this century. Signs point to vertical cities and flying
> suburbs – little airport communities 100 miles and more from

skyscraper clusters rising in the midst of acres of parks and play-grounds.

So having brought the molten iron to the surface, it then needs to make it up to the flying suburbs. Or perhaps they mean that these are suburbs from which people fly into the city. Or maybe both.

If it is indeed the former though, there's yet another problem to be faced.

> ... window walls will slip down in slots to merge outdoors with indoors in favorable weather ...

That's going to be some hazard in one of those flying suburban houses. Dad returns home from work in his jet pack thinking the living room walls have been opened because it's a nice sunny day only to fly straight into a huge pane of glass and slide down it in the best of cartoon traditions.

Jane Dobson's house of the future, also envisaged from 1950, is very much on terra firma and it doesn't even need to run a pipe down to the centre of the earth for its heating.

> This Dobson air-conditioned house is not a prefabricated struc-ture, though all its parts are mass-produced. Metal, sheets of plastic and aerated clay are cut to size on the spot. In the center of this eight-room house is a unit that contains all the utilities; air-conditioning apparatus, plumbing, bathrooms, showers, electric range, electric outlets. Around this central unit the house has been pieced together. Some of it is poured plastic, the floors, for instance. By 2000, wood, brick and stone are ruled out because they are too expensive. It is a cheap house. With all its furnishings, Joe Dobson paid only $5000 for it. Though it is galeproof and weatherproof, it is built to last only about 25 years. Nobody in 2000 sees any sense in building a house that will last a century.

No doubt after reading that stockbrokers the world over rushed to their phones shouting, 'buy, buy, buy, wood, brick or stone, the price is going to go through the mass produced aerated clay roof'.

Just to be clear then, you start with the unit that controls everything and, on the spot, cut to size all the floors, ceiling and walls that are then pieced together around it to make this eight roomed house.

Wouldn't it be easier to have standard sizes and build the house that way, which, in effect would be like making a giant Lego house (which has now been done by Mr James May and friends)? In fact, if you want to see the world that Jane Dobson was predicted to be living in, just go to Legoland, though if you happen to be travelling in time from the Fifties to do so, be warned, the price they said a house would cost today will only just get you a family day ticket, and that wouldn't include popcorn or entrance to the life size Lego Jane Dobson exhibit.

Other great selling points of this flat packed home are the fact that it is both galeproof *and* weatherproof – clearly gales aren't included in the set of things that form the weather – and its 25-year life span. Presumably this is factored in such that 25 years to the day after it was erected, the house collapses. The owners would have been warned though as when they opened the packaging the components of the house came in, a recorded voice would have said, 'this house will self-destruct in twenty five years'.

Finally the magnificent coup de grace that no one will want a house that lasts a century. No one! Absolutely no one! Such certainty, such absolutism, such nonsense!

From Legoland to Disneyland where, in 1957, they built the Monsanto House of the Future which was predicted to appear in 1986 and continued to eschew the virtues of bricks and mortar, proudly proclaiming:

The floors on which you are walking, the gently sloping walls around you, and even the ceilings are made of plastics.

Why the walls should be gently sloping is something of a mystery, but looking down from above, the house basically resembled a large white plus sign, perhaps a subliminal statement about what a marvellous addition to the landscape it was going to be.

Of course, it was picked up by *Popular Mechanics* magazine – they weren't going to miss out on this scoop – who described it by saying:

Futuristic models sprout wings where you need them.

Well, no, they're not wings and they're predominantly at right angles to each other, but as attention grabbing headlines go, it does the job.

Excitedly, the magazine also stated that:

The preliminary design has been completed at the Massachusetts Institute of Technology. A scale model will go up some time this spring. A life size test house may be ready in a year.

No doubt there were many who could barely contain themselves, especially as the magazine went on to further entice its readers by adding:

What will happen after that is anybody's guess.

Well with the benefit of hindsight and historical fact we can take the guesswork out of the equation; the house was taken down and removed from Disneyland in 1967, it didn't even spread its wings and fly away. At the end of the day it was all just a bit Mickey Mouse.

The Monsanto House of the Future 1957–67. R.I.P.

Moving into the Sixties, the *Chicago Tribune* ran an article entitled, 'An Expert Foresees Startling Changes in Housing in Year 2000', in which the so called expert predicted that by the turn of the century many houses would be 'demountable'.

At first glance you might think by this the author means it'll be possible to saddle houses up like horses, ride them around and then demount them, which actually is not too far from the truth, apart from the part about saddling them up and riding them around.

Here's what he actually meant.

Our homes will move with us when we change locations, just as our furniture does today. The house will be assembled of interlocking room units, each with its own thermo-electric heating, cooling, and lighting system built into the walls.

It's great. No need to book a hotel when you go on holiday, just pack up the house and take it with you; might be difficult getting it into a suitcase though.

Mind you, among this merciless mocking, we should mention modern ventures like the Pod House – a structure that is literally delivered to a site and is ready to go as a dwelling. While you don't do the 'packing up and delivery' it does kind of bear a passing resemblance to our expert's vision, so you can't say we're not being balanced (well, you can say it, but we can't hear you, so there's no point, is there?).

The legendary Century 21 Exposition took place in Seattle in 1962, a world fair that promised a future of delightful innovation, nowhere more so than in its programme, which was clearly written by someone on acid.

> In a shimmer of golden light, you enter the World of Century 21. It is a rainbow-hued world of cubed facades … optimistic, yet realistically aware of present-day threats.

Make that two, possibly three tabs of acid and a magic mushroom chaser.

> Then comes a burst of yellow-golden summer sunlight and a home unlike any other you have seen appears. You notice the indoor swimming pool and garden, the private heliport, the way your home of tomorrow rotates to take advantage of the sun. You marvel at the slip-proof bathroom, wall to wall television and flick-of-the switch windows.

Something's not quite right here. You only *notice* the indoor pool and garden, the heliport and the rotating home, yet when it comes to the slip-proof bathroom, you're bloody *marvelling*. It's as if being able to take a bath without fear of tripping over and banging your head was seen as the height of technological advance in the early Sixties.

As for that rotation, with the sun disappearing in and out of the clouds in Britain, your poor home would be spinning like a top in no time. Meal times would be a nightmare and that slip-proof bathroom had better be as marvellous as it's made out to be; if it's not up to par, a sudden shift in the direction of the sunlight and you'll go flying headlong out of the shower before you can say, 'I haven't washed my armpits yet.'

But something is missing from this incredible house of the future. What could it possibly be? To the Expo programme again prediction hunters!

'Does it have a radar controlled supersonic, neutronic fission freezer?' says a woman's voice. Ye Gods, these folk from the past don't expect much do they? Well, does it have a radar controlled supersonic neutronic (whatever that might be) fission freezer?

'I'm not wise enough to predict all the inventions of tomorrow,' comes the answer. And there it is, the understatement of this and every other time period. If only they'd replaced the word 'all' with the words 'any of' it would have made perfect sense.

A decade on and an architect and inventor chappie by the name of R. Buckminster Fuller thought he'd cracked the weighty issue of over-population in the future with his plan for something called Tetra or Tetrahedron City. The idea was described in a book called *49 Cities* as follows:

Tetra city was to be a floating or land-based residential pyramid that could grow to accommodate one million inhabitants. The building was to have 'three triangular walls of 5,000 living units apiece,' 200-stories tall with two-mile long walls at its base. Large openings in the structure would occur every fifty stories, allowing sunlight to enter the public garden at the bottom of the interior. Three city centers would rim the structure at different levels. Each of these featured 'a community park, complete with lagoon, palms and shopping center in geodesic domes.'

It's ambitious, but perhaps before embarking on this project he should really have considered this; why on earth would anyone want to live in a gigantic floating pyramid along with 999,999 other people? It's a small point, but somewhat relevant, especially given the fact that statistically, a fair proportion of those people – your new neighbours – are going to be deeply irritating.

Then of course there's Egypt's experience with pyramids to consider. Surely the fundamental lesson to learn is that once inside, it's virtually impossible to find your way out again. Those million people are going to be kicking themselves when, after buying one of Tetra City's bijou living units, they discover that they can never leave. It's Hotel California all over again.

193RD STOREY LIVING UNIT IN TETRA CITY AVAILABLE

....

These well-presented, compact properties include a number of original features and benefit from:

- **Hundreds of thousands of neighbours.**
- **Curses if any items are removed from the pyramid.**
- **Sea sickness tablet cabinets** *(exclusive to floating versions).*
- **No need ever to sharpen razor blades.**
- **Mummified remains of ancient rulers.**

Viewing recommended though you won't be able to find your way out of the pyramid if you do view the property so you might as well buy it.

Incredibly designs were drawn up for Tetra City and imagined pictures were taken, some of which were shown in 2007 at New York's Museum of Modern Art in an exhibition entitled 75 Years of Architecture.

One picture, based on a design by Fuller and a Japanese architect called Shoji Sadao, depicts the enormous pyramid floating in Tokyo Bay and, to say it's a blot on the landscape would be playing things down a little. It *is* the fucking landscape! It dominates to such an extent that Mount Fuji, Japan's highest mountain, looks as if it's rapidly developing an inferiority complex. Tutankhamun eat your heart out.

The text accompanying the picture describes the pyramidal city much as above, adding, 'Fuller . . . spent his career searching for "ever higher performance with ever less investment of material resources."' It's not hard to figure out why Fuller got 'ever less investment of material resources' for this particular project.

The text continues detailing this great feat of architectural prediction before ending as follows: 'Fuller and Sadao's radical urban proposal was never built.'

Surprising that.

7. Trailer trash

Despite their weird and wonderful features, all the marvellous homes predicted above have one thing in common; none of them are able to be driven.

This might come as a surprise to economist and entrepreneur Roger W. Babson because back in 1935, possibly while at the wheel of a Buick 67c Convertible Resat Rod, he said quite authoritatively that,

> Within twenty years, more than half the population of the United States will be living in automobile trailers!

In 1955 the population of America was 166 million, which means that, if Roger was correct, over 83 million people should have been motoring around in their trailer homes.

He was ever so slightly completely and utterly wrong.

LEISURE AND ENTERTAINMENT

Leisure is generally defined as: 'time when a person is not at work, plus time when they are not performing household or other daily chores.' Over the years certain members of society have opined that this definition should also include; 'time when a person *is* at work but is not being spied upon by their boss or some other officious pen-pusher who'll totally unreasonably grass them up for not doing what they're being paid to do, plus time when they're *supposed* to be performing household or other daily chores, but are furtively doing something else', with the emphasis very much on 'furtively'.

Whichever way you look at it, leisure time is there to be filled, so crucial choices must be made. For example, should that spare three hours be spent visiting a library of repute and cramming one's mind full of wisdom, both ancient and modern? Or should it be passed buying a multi-pack of Stella and heading down the high street in search of some likely lads to have it out with?

It's a tough one and it's not made any easier by the fact that, in recent years, leisure options have multiplied exponentially. Along with the more traditional distractions of hobbies, correspondence courses and illegally copied films, today there are thousands of TV channels, internet sites, computer games and mobile phone apps.

Choices await us at every twist and turn, and indeed bend and chicane. If a caveman (or woman) were to stomp into one of today's leisure centres for instance, not only would they receive dirty looks for clubbing the coffee-machinasaurus to pieces, they'd also be bamboozled by the sheer number and variety of activities on offer – not to mention the fact that the explanation of the '3 for 2' day passes promotion might result in them murdering the person on reception, quite probably with just cause.

As someone once said, or possibly plagiarised from someone else, 'so much to do, so little time', and, had it been a prediction about leisure time of the future, it would have been pretty much spot on. Sadly, it wasn't, but perhaps if those from the past who did make predictions about free time of the future hadn't done so in quite such a leisurely fashion, they'd have more of it to spend feeling deeply embarrassed about how very wrong they were.

1. Fashionistas, frocks and faux pas

Predicting fashion trends is vital if you want to be thought of as both fashionable and on trend, less so if you're happy to look like a sack of potatoes, though the chances are looking like a sack of potatoes will be very 'in' next season.

For those who do want their image to scream stylish and up-to-the-minute though, turning up to a party wearing burgundy when everyone knows that prune is the new burgundy screams something very different, something like: 'aaaaarrggghhhhh, I'll never be able to go out again, my life is over, I'll never be thought of as cool, I may as well admit to liking Phil Collins and be done with it'.

Of course, predicting long-term fashion trends is less important for that party next week, but if you want to cut a dash at the old age home tombola night when you're 90, it's absolutely essential.

And fashion predictions are not just made for elderly outfit planning. There's cash to be made here too. If your fashion house can correctly predict what is going to be 'in' in five years' time, then you will be the ones to rake in the dollars.

Fashion though is such a strange game; clothes of the past always look weird while clothes of 'the future' always look ... weird. Perhaps the true answer is to devise a timeless set of garments that governments all over the world agree to make their citizens wear for at least the next hundred years. That way couture would be secure and no one would have to rush around second guessing what boots might be trendy 20 years hence.

But you can't keep a good old fashion predictor down, so thanks must go to the lovely people at Pathetone who, in 1939, provided a much-needed glimpse into the future of fashion with one of their legendary 'Pathetone Weekly' films. In this marvellous piece entitled 'The Spice of Variety – EVE, AD 2000!' the Pathetone crew donned their haute couture hats of prediction and set about telling all and sundry what fashion would be like at the end of the millennium. It began with:

One idea is a dress that can be adapted for morning, afternoon and evening.

It's a great idea, especially as most women do change their outfits twice a day (three times on weekends and Bank Holidays). But how is it possible you holler? Don't worry, the film reveals all, albeit with a large helping of traditional 1930s cheese.

It's the sleeves what does it.

And then to illustrate, a woman, quite possibly a lady-in-waiting, unzips and reverses the sleeve of a dress worn by another woman. Fantastically, we then see exactly the same dress, only with different coloured sleeves, which, rather than wow people in the year 2000 is far more likely to get them saying, 'Hang on a minute. That's the same dress you wore this morning only you're now wearing it inside out.'

Clearly, in order to avoid social suicide, it would be better to ensure that when wearing this dress, you try not to run into any of the people who saw you wearing a previous adaptation of it, in which case, you might as well just keep the same outfit on all day.

Moving on, the film also foresees the end of the road for a favourite staple of women's attire.

> ... another designer goes so far as to believe that skirts will disappear entirely.

To be clear, this designer isn't suggesting that ladies of 2000 will wear invisible skirts, rather that skirts will no longer exist. Either way he was wrong, as he was when he went on to add that,

> ... an electric belt will adapt the body to climatic changes.

Disappointingly, instead of the accompanying image being one of a woman walking into a storm and an umbrella suddenly shooting out from her snood, or racing through a blizzard with an igloo miraculously popping out of her earrings, the image depicts a woman attempting to walk up some steps as a howling gale pushes her back. Quite what the belt is actually doing to help in this situation is not entirely clear, but as a future fashion statement it was one for the off-cuts bin.

Other designer innovations expected were wedding gowns made of glass and a dress made of aluminium with a sash to change it for afternoon or evenings. This latter creation also comes with a very interesting accessory; an electric headlight, which the narrator, now in cheese overload, tells us is, 'to help her to find an honest man'. This is quite literally an electric light bulb on a stick pushed through the woman's hair and the real reason she has it is never made clear, perhaps it lights up every time she has a good idea.

Having spent most of the time focusing on women, the film briefly, and in somewhat derogatory fashion, switches to men.

> As for him, if he matters at all, there won't be any shaving, collars, ties or pockets.

We're then shown a gentleman with a large goatee beard trussed up in a sort of jumpsuit with a circular antennae type thing on his head, which, presumably is something to do with the telephone stuck to the middle of his chest.

> He'll be fitted with a telephone, a radio and containers for coins, keys and candies for cuties.

Seems somewhat odd to forgo pockets, and then replace them with containers which are basically pocket-like only bulkier.

Nice also to see that alliteration was alive and well in the Thirties, it's just a shame that in those more austere days they couldn't add 'his cock' to the list.

While Pathetone predicted adaptable clothing, the editors of *Changing Times* magazine went a step further in their January 1961 edition, foreseeing that a 'Big Seller' in 1975, would be:

> Disposable clothing, made of paper but not looking like paper ... available at low prices for children, garage men, factory workers, housewives and home handymen.

A strange and rather specific conglomeration of people there who will all no doubt be relieved that their outfits won't actually look like paper, though hopefully it will still be possible to write on them, something that could even spell the end of annoying, hand-held shopping lists.

Changing Times magazine is now known as *Kiplinger's Personal Finance* and prides itself, apparently, on giving 'sound, unbiased advice in clear, concise language'.

The founder of the magazine, coincidentally a Mr Kiplinger, also said that:

> The times will always be changing. Much of life and work consists of looking for the changes in advance and figuring out what to do about them.

Well, in this case that's ignoring them because they never happened; is that sound, unbiased, clear and concise enough?

Five years later though and it was *Life* magazine's turn to herald a new era of paper fashion garments.

> Paper apparel's real pioneers, after years of speaking into deaf ears, are now talking ebulliently about a boundless future.

They went on to quote a Ronald Bard as saying:

> Five years from now 75% of the population will be wearing disposable clothing.

Bard was vice-president of a family firm previously devoted to making only stretch tights for women and children. He was clearly desperate to find something else to focus his attentions on because he went on to say that,

> In paper you are only limited by your imagination.

Yes indeed, and the rain. And bending over too quickly. And children, possibly in stretch tights, with crayons.

Next to laud paper petticoats and the like was an Elisa Daggs who said:

> Paper needs its own architecture. Sealing machines will replace sewing machines.

Maybe the sealing machines could seal the mouths of anyone who started making outlandish paper-clothes predictions.

Finally the article quoted textile designer Julian Tomchin, who, when speaking about using paper for garments said,

> It's right for our age, after all who is going to do laundry in space?

Most people who work in launderettes quite probably, given the option of spending the next 20 years doing service washes on the high street or washing astronauts' smalls while hurtling round the galaxy at warp factor 9.

Back on Earth, sort of, Julian goes on to predict how he sees things developing in the paper-clothes market.

> Mr Tomchin also believes that improved techniques will bring prices down until garments will be packaged in tear-off rolls, like sandwich bags, and sold for pennies.

It's a cracking idea, but fraught with dangers. If things got confused, you could get into a situation where you wipe up spilt juice with a dress and go to a party wearing a single sheet of kitchen roll.

Perhaps the last fashionable words should be left to the legendary, Coco Chanel, who on seeing a brand new clothing item known as the 'miniskirt,' declared, in 1966, that:

> It's a bad joke that won't last. Not with winter coming.

Well, she should Coco.

2. Would you credit it?

When writing on the subject of money authors can sometimes be carried along on a giant tidal wave of optimism and, on occasion, delight their readers with statements about the possibility of a future where money will not play such a big and enslaving part in our lives. One such gentleman was John Langdon-Davies who, in his seminal 1936 text – *A Short History of the Future* – enticingly stated that:

> If we are to begin to try and understand life as it will be in 1960, we must begin by realizing that food, clothing and shelter will cost as little as air.

It might be better to try and understand what the bally hell was going on inside his head because in general, air is free, hence we must presume that John is suggesting the cost of food, clothing and shelter will be nothing. Zilch, zero, nada, bugger all.

Ironically, as a prediction, it's rich in the extreme, though it's possible that its intentions were good and that John hoped great abundance would reign such that no one ever need go hungry and homeless again. Sadly, in this day and age the only people who get free stuff are celebrities, though at least they really appreciate receiving it.

In fact the way things are going it's far more likely the inverse will be true because as governments find new and inventive ways to tax our decaying atmosphere, in the future air will probably cost as much as food, clothing and shelter, which are increasingly prohibitively expensive.

Langdon-Davies' prediction was remarkable not only because of quite how optimistic it was, but also because just a few short years previously the world had found itself reeling from the financial tsunami that was the crash of 1929 (we'll get to that shortly).

By 1931, with America in pretty dire straits after the financial meltdown the *New York Times* attempted to cheer everyone up by asking several prominent thinkers to look ahead 80 years and predict what life would be like. (*The New York Times* was celebrating its 80th anniversary in 1931, thus the somewhat arbitrary 80 years hence, though given the prevailing economic conditions, celebrating might not be the right word.)

One of these great minds was physicist and inventor Michael Pupin who, for reasons known only to him, chose to consider not physics, rather the plight of the world's finances. In his opinion the outlook for most people was pretty good.

This civilization is the greatest material achievement of applied science during this memorable period. Its power for creating wealth was never equaled in human history. But it lacks the wisdom of distributing equitably the wealth which it creates. One can safely prophesy that during the next eighty years this civilization will correct this deficiency by creating an industrial democracy which will guarantee to the worker an equitable share in the work produced by his work.

In essence what Mike is saying is that over the ensuing 80 years the world will become wiser and with that wisdom will come equality. Well, in the great battle of human traits, stupidity has well and truly whupped wisdom's ass, handing disproportionate wealth to the likes of Donald Trump and his fully autonomous hairdo. The workers are revolted.

Back in the 1930s, if you didn't have cash to spend during your leisure time you might have been a little stuck, unless you were prepared to borrow from the local loan shark at such exorbitant interest rates your descendants would still be paying off his descendants today.

Thank goodness then that in 1950, the founder of Diner's club, Frank McNamara, invented the credit card. Suddenly a whole world of leisure and entertainment opened up to the masses who could now afford to go and see the latest films or buy a new tennis racket and feel as if they'd paid nothing, and possibly continue to pay nothing, that is, until the bailiffs turned up at their door and took most of their possessions.

By 1977 spending on credit cards was, to put it mildly, rampant, a reason for the credit card companies to rejoice, you, and most sensible people might think. Not so according to Ray Zablocki. An economist at the Stanford Research Institute, Zablocki was convinced that the credit card companies had got themselves in too deep; they were shelling out vast sums of money while their card holders were paying off as little as possible. On the face of it, too much out and too little in makes the credit card company's situation seem, to use a complex financial term, screwed. Zablocki therefore speculated:

> By 1980 losses on credit cards will overwhelm the industry and they will become extinct.

Unfortunately for Ray his credit rating might be good, but his credit card prediction rating is zero.

3. *Wall Street comes tumbling down (Part 1)*

To enjoy one's leisure time and take part in activities beyond those that are free (and often crap), money does tend to come in handy. And in order to have some, it can be useful to listen to what those in the know have to say about shares, investments and the 4:15 at Aintree.

Many a stock-picker, pension plotter or Bernie Madoff have earned a decent crust by predicting what's going to happen in the financial markets. Well, Bernie just nicked it, but his spreadsheets looked ever so good. Others, though, have not done so well and it is to these types that we must now venture.

At times of great panic, it seems that for some reason, otherwise well-informed and reasonable thinkers part company with their grasps on reality and start spouting the most outlandish nonsense, often in the face of overwhelming evidence to the contrary. The Crash of 1929 is a shining example of this phenomenon.

In the years leading up to it, many economists made bullish predictions that flew in the face of past experience and, though these forecasts might have been meant to reassure the public, they actually resulted in the predictor's stock plummeting within a few short years. For example, here's John Maynard Keynes in 1927.

We will not have any more crashes in our time.

If by 'our time' he meant the five minutes after he'd committed this sentence to paper then he would have been correct. As a piece of international long term financial speculation, it was quite the opposite. This woefully wrong prediction didn't harm his career though, which goes to show that you can miss one of the most acute economic meltdowns of the 20th century and still have a whole school of macro-economics named after you.

Two months before the crash, with the US economy already decidedly jittery, leading US economist Irving Fisher was intent on soothing people's nerves and foretold in *the New York Times* of 5 September 1929, that:

There may be a recession in stock prices, but not anything in the nature of a crash.

Anyone who took Fisher's statement to heart and decided not to sell would have been seriously disheartened and seriously broke when the shit finally hit the fan on 24 October. On this day, known in the US as 'Black Thursday', and because of the time difference, 'Black Friday', in Europe (and for some reason Purple Monday in Bogota), there was a complete collapse of share prices on the New York Stock Exchange – a truly seismic event. It caused more than a few ripples of intense panic round the world, yet there were some who claimed people were over-reacting. Unbelievably on the very day of the collapse, Arthur Reynolds – the Chairman of Continental Illinois Bank of Chicago – reassured his customers and the wider world:

This crash is not going to have much effect on business.

One assumes he said this because he was shit-scared about his job prospects and the nice Californian farm he planned to buy on retirement, but it singularly failed in its attempt at reassurance and in the days that followed, things just got worse. A short while later with the collapse still unfolding and most sentient financiers reaching for their stash of cyanide, Paul Block, President of the Block Newspaper Chain, echoed Arthur Reynolds' sentiments and claimed that:

In most of the cities and towns of this country, this Wall Street panic will have no effect.

If those towns and cities were in Lala land, he might have been right – though even there property prices did suffer slightly – but if he was referring to conurbations in the dimension known as reality, then he was way off the mark and should have been tarred, feathered and run out of those very cities and towns with his tail between his legs.

By the end of 1929, the economic world was in a very different place to where it had been at the beginning of the year and millions looked to the start of the new decade with dread and foreboding. Not so the jaunty secretary to the US Treasury, Andrew W. Mellon. Maybe ridiculous optimism is a fate that befalls everyone who possesses a misspelled fruit surname, because Mellon had it in farm loads. On the very last day of 1929, he gave vent to his trouble-free ruminations:

> I see nothing in the present situation that is either menacing or
> warrants pessimism. ... I have every confidence that there will be
> a revival of activity in the spring, and that during this coming year
> the country will make steady progress.

Talk about a glass half full. Andrew's flagon of Mellon juice was
positively overflowing.

Spring 1930 arrived and with it came the green shoots of
new blooms, but not sadly of recovery. That didn't deter Julius
Barnes, the head of Hoover's National Business Survey Conference though. He made the following declaration on 16
March:

> The spring of 1930 marks the end of a period of grave concern.
> ... American business is steadily coming back to a normal level of
> prosperity.

It would take until 1954 for the American stock market to
return to its pre-1929 crash position. Julius' prediction was only
correct in sense that an end is also a beginning.

4. Wall Street comes tumbling down (Part 2)

One would have hoped that on hearing the succession of
hopeless pronouncements made by bankers, financiers and
economists *before* the crash of 1929, someone somewhere
would have had the nous to predict that in future we really
shouldn't listen to their ilk again. Unfortunately if such an
astute person existed, they were not listened to and consequently those in control of our money continued to make
erroneous predictions, throughout the 20th century.

But it was in the first decade of the 21st century that we
really got our fingers burnt, or to put it in slightly harsher
terms; the entire world banking system nearly collapsed. It was
in the area of sub-prime mortgages that the troubles originated,

more specifically, mortgage lenders lending money to people who did not have the means to pay them back. Several voices in the economic jungle did make a noise about this problem but more often than not their voices were drowned out by the Big Beasts of Finance – who insisted that all was fine and dandy in Mortgage Land.

Unfortunately it wasn't. It was getting into an ever-worsening shape, with incorrect pricing of risk posing a very serious problem. This 'credit crunch' led to American banking 'liquidity' problems and a world recession in 2008, seen by many as the most severe economic crisis since that sparked by the crash of 1929. But even though the signs were there well before the housing bubble burst, many working in the heart of America's real estate, mortgage-loan and banking system repeatedly reassured the public that all was hunky dory.

Take, Mr David Lereah, Chief Economist of the National Association of Realtors. In 2006, he confidently stated:

> The good news is that inventory levels are improving and housing supply will come closer to buyer demand in 2006. We expect a healthy and more balanced market next year.

Which set of figures he was studying is anyone's guess but his upbeat assessment was endorsed by former Treasury Secretary Hank Paulson, who, in April 2007, weighed in with this prediction:

> I don't see [sub-prime mortgage market troubles] imposing a serious problem. I think it's going to be largely contained.

If ever a financial crisis wasn't contained, it was the one about to explode. And throwing his hat into the ring of calm waters was head of AIG financial products, Joseph Cassano, who in August 2007, proclaimed:

It is hard for us, without being flippant, to even see a scenario within any kind of realm of reason that would see us losing one dollar in any of these [credit default swap] transactions.

Three big cheeses; three stinky predictions.

In the aftermath of the crisis, the US senate issued the Levin-Coburn Report which forensically examined the reasons the crash had taken place. It highlighted the failure of:

... the market itself to rein in the excesses of Wall Street.

After this hard-hitting document hit the Senate, there were those who predicted that excess on Wall Street would now become a thing of the past; they really did. But as various governments talked the talk about punishing those who instigated the crash (but walked the walk of completely leaving them alone while still sharing power lunches and planning the world's next economic disaster with them) it seems that these predictors were as wrong as Lereah, Paulson and Cassano.

5. Pass the popcorn

In February 1895 the Lumière brothers, Auguste and Louis patented the first ever film camera or cinematographé as they would have called it seeing as how they were French. Shortly afterwards they screened the first ever film entitled *Sortie des Usines Lumière à Lyon* or *Workers Leaving the Lumière Factory*. It was a complex multi-layered black comedy, but in essence it showed workers leaving the Lumière factory. Whether such an epic would get green-lit by one of today's Hollywood studios remains open to question, but in one fell swoop Gusty and Lulu had opened up a whole new world of leisure possibilities.

Not that they were convinced of that though. Rather the opposite in fact, as this 1895 prediction from Auguste would suggest.

> My invention ... can be exploited for a certain time as a scientific curiosity, but apart from that it has no commercial value whatsoever.

And just in case anyone missed the point, he made it absolutely clear by also saying,

> The cinema is an invention without any future.

This is an extreme example of someone being pessimistic about a brilliant money-making device (one that would go on to make thousands of millions for those involved in the movie industry) that they themselves had created.

Cinema of course did have a future and rather a good one at that. Indeed, it rapidly became a very popular way for people to spend their leisure time. All this was despite the fact that the films were silent; consequently, the race was on to find a way of being able to hear what the actors were actually saying.

At the forefront of this race was inventor extraordinaire, Thomas Edison, who in 1913 came up with the kinetophone, an early sound-synch apparatus. Sadly, it was rubbish, which could explain why he made the following prediction.

> The talking motion picture will not supplant the regular silent motion picture. There is such a tremendous investment to pantomime pictures that it would be absurd to disturb it.

Perhaps it might have been better for him if he'd said that on a silent film so that no one would have heard it.

Around the same time, a young English fellow named Charlie Chaplin was beginning a career that would see him become the world's first real movie superstar. By 1916 he was given the princely sum of $670,000 to produce and star in his own films, yet it seemed as far as he was concerned, it was money not particularly well spent. Said Chaplin:

> The cinema is little more than a fad. It's canned drama. What audiences really want to see is flesh and blood on the stage.

He was right in one respect; audiences *do* like to see flesh and blood (plenty of each if possible) but they're more than happy to see it on a screen where there's much less chance of them being hit by a stray eyeball.

Chaplin's comments are all the more remarkable because just a year earlier the highest grossing film of the silent era, *Birth of a Nation*, had been released. It made about $10 million, a pretty penny in those days, and its director, D.W. Griffith is regarded as one of the first, true greats. Chaplin called him, 'the teacher of us all', and Orson Welles said, '... no art form owes so much to a single man'. Strange then that in 1924 Griffith came out with this target-missing arrow:

> Speaking movies are impossible. When a century has passed, all thought of so-called speaking movies will have been abandoned. It will never be possible to synchronize the voice with the picture.

Three years later the first 'talkie' *The Jazz Singer* hit the screens and Mr Griffith probably wished he could crawl into a large hole. But his most famous pupil, Charlie C, was still getting all antsy about 'Talkies'.

> Moving pictures need sound as much as Beethoven symphonies need lyrics.

This was possibly because he had found his home in silent films and wanted to protect their future. Or maybe he just didn't like change. A third possibility is that he'd trained everyone in his family and all of his friends and acquaintances to communicate with each other silently, in which case it would be baffling for them to watch a screen with people making weird, indecipherable noises.

Our old friend Thomas Edison had his own take on this new and exciting cinematic development.

> People will tire of talkers. Talking is no substitute for the good acting we had in silent pictures.

Probably best to stick to light bulbs Tommy boy.

As cinema's tentacles multiplied and spread through the globe, hooking in ever higher numbers of paying audiences, some individuals stood back and were awed by the phenomenal possibilities of the film-making world. One of these was poet and beat-box-star-before-its-time, John Betjeman who, in 1935, declared,

> Colour and stereoscopy will make cinema into the greatest art in the world. Bad films will be impossible.

Battlefield Earth, Sex Lives of the Potato Men, Gigli, Ishtar. Great art? No.

By the mid 1960s the silent versus talkie debate had been well and truly won and the only people making silent films any more were people called Hugo, who wore black crew neck sweaters, lived in an attic flat on the left bank of the Seine and ate pebbles. But wouldn't you know it, with cinema approaching the heyday of its heyday's heyday, along comes a deep thinker to predict its downfall.

The particular deep thinker in question here was anarchist art critic Sir Herbert Read who, writing in a May 1964 *New Scientist* magazine article entitled 'Atrophied Muscles and Empty Art', set out his position. He was certain that:

> Passive entertainment will fill ever expanding periods of non-employment.

Notice the way he refers to 'non-employment,' rather than

'un-employment' – he would have made a great spin doctor. In Read's future (he was talking about 1984), heavy cultural shifts would occur and movies would be hit very hard:

> Cinemas will have disappeared because it requires less effort to view the same kind of programme on the television screen.

Yes it does, though it's not much of a date. The young adolescent boy of the early Sixties is hardly going to win over his true love by inviting her over to watch *Ben Hur* on a small, black and white telly while his Mum does her knitting in the armchair.

But if going to the cinema was too much effort for the yoof of the day what did Herbie think they'd spend their time doing?

> ... younger people will crowd into dives where they can expend their unused energies in dancing like dervishes to the jazz bands.

Of course. Jazz. The perfect antidote to those atrophied muscles. A bit of free form improvisation never fails to bring out the dervish in anyone.

With all of these arguments about the future of cinema it's a miracle that anybody had any time to actually *make* any films. But they did, and some of them went on to do awfully well. Yet again though, there were those within the gilded halls of Hollywood, who still managed to put a downer on things and predict disastrous consequences for a whole raft of projects.

Back in 1926 for instance, Louis B. Mayer was pitched the idea of a film about a new, child-friendly cartoon mouse. The MGM boss predicted its failure because,

> Every woman is frightened of a mouse.

That's arguable, but let's not forget most people are scared of having their heads and limbs violently chopped off, but that doesn't stop them paying top dollar to watch films about chain-saw wielding maniacs.

Being terrifically wrong wasn't just the domain of the big bosses though. With a touch of dashing insouciance, Gary Cooper, on being offered the role of Rhett Butler in a new film called *Gone with the Wind*, turned it down, saying:

> *Gone with the Wind* is going to be the biggest flop in cinema history. I'm just glad it'll be Clark Gable who's falling on his face and not Gary Cooper.

Note the bloated, Caesar-like use of the third person and also the fact that *Gone with the Wind* is one of the most popular films of all time.

Gary's career didn't suffer too badly though, and he ended up playing a street-smart cowboy in a fair few Westerns, which is odd given his great capacity to shoot himself in the foot.

Another gargantuan movie success was the 1972 picture, *The Godfather*. This is a film that splits people into two groups – the divide being between those who love the film and those who are perturbed by the notion of someone sharing a bed with a dead horse's head. There was obviously something about the film in development that caused people to make all sorts of woefully incorrect predictions about the cast and director.

Speaking in 1970, Francis Ford Coppola (who went on to direct the film) revealed that:

> Paramount ... want me to direct a hunk of trash. I don't want to do it. I want to do art films.

Good job he eventually left those to Sofia.

And when the film finally did get the go ahead, a Paramount studio executive was quite categorical about the film's lead part:

I assure you, Marlon Brando will not appear in this film.

That's one studio executive whose career was soon to be sleeping with the fishes.

6. Where's the bloody remote?

Lee De Forest was an interesting chap. He was heavily involved in the early days of radio, competing with Marconi and working with among others, the US military. With over 180 patents to his name, you could say he was something of a one-man inventions wizard. At least, that's the way he saw it as evinced by his modestly titled autobiography *Father of Radio*. Yes, in spite of a wealth of evidence pointing to the involvement of others in the creation of the wireless, De Forest viewed it as being pretty much his own work. This was nowhere more graphically highlighted than when he asked a group of radio executives (well after the medium was up and running): 'What have you gentlemen done with my child?' Although some of them exhibited panic about a potential paternity suit, De Forest went on to scathingly add: 'The radio was conceived as a potent instrumentality for culture, fine music, the uplifting of America's mass intelligence. You have debased this child, you have sent him out in the streets in rags of ragtime, tatters of jive and boogie-woogie, to collect money from all and sundry.'

Given these very stringent views on the commercialisation of culture on the radio, when the talk in media circles turned to the big new beast called television, it was hardly a surprise when Lee got well overheated. Did the 'Father of radio' like the concept of TV? No he did not – he saw it as the devil's post-watershed spawn and he was having none of it. In fact, by 1926, he was utterly convinced that radio would win the day, with telly coming so far behind it shouldn't even bother turning up at the starting line:

> While theoretically and technically television may be feasible, commercially and financially it is an impossibility, a development of which we need waste little time dreaming.

It seems De Forest and Auguste Lumière were cut from very similar cloth; perhaps he was so mired in radio, when it came to television he couldn't see de forest for the trees. (Apologies.) Interestingly for a man so opposed to moving pictures being swept into the nation's homes, his fourth wife, Marie Mosquini, was a motion picture actress. She survived him and probably went on to watch as many TV programmes as she could in their living room, delighted not to have him berating her about the superior merits of radio.

Come 2 November 1936, John Logie Baird oversaw the world's first official television transmission at London's Alexandra Palace. A momentous event in most people's eyes, but there were others whose feathers were well and truly ruffled by it. Writing in *The Listener*, Rex Lambert rather snootily declared:

> Television won't matter in your lifetime or mine.

And what was Mr Lambert's job? Editor of the *Radio Times* no less, which, at the time really was a radio listings magazine. How horrified would Lambert have been when the magazine started including TV listings as well?

In the aftermath of Logie Baird's broadcast and the realisation that television was here to stay, its opponents started cobbling together scare-mongering stories and warnings about the evil new medium. The *New York Times* in 1939 declared that because people had to glue their eyes to the TV screen they wouldn't have much time for it. What did they think of people gluing their ears to radio sets then? Weren't they being a bit selective in their chastisements?

This 'glue' analogy took root in some people's minds and led to a whole plethora of anti-TV terms and phrases; 'goggle box,' 'your eyes will go square,' etc.; terms largely made up by sour people who worked in radio and felt upstaged by the television bastards who were muscling in on their turf. However, it wasn't only the radio bods foaming at the mouth. Daryl Zanuck of Twentieth Century Fox waited a full ten years after the Alexandra Palace broadcast to denounce television.

Television won't last because people will soon get tired of staring at a plywood box every night.

Maybe no one told him that the place to look wasn't the box's surround, but the screen positioned in its centre. Perhaps he spent evenings gazing at the *back* of the box, wondering what all of the fuss was about. Or could it be that on the same day a brand new television showed up at his place, a plywood box was also delivered and he got the two mixed up, watching the plywood box for hours on end and cutting up the TV set to make some nice shelves? (To be fair though, staring at a plywood box is preferable to watching a lot of today's TV shows as anyone who has had the misfortune to see *OMG! With Peaches Geldof* will surely agree.)

Whatever the case, most people trampled all over Zanuck's thesis and proved themselves more than happy to glue their square eyes to the box for hours on end.

However, a voice was raised that supported Zanuck. In 1948, Mary Somerville stated that:

Television won't last. It's a flash in the pan.

Strangely negative, especially given that Mary was one of tele-vision's first big stars. Oh no, hang on, she wasn't; she was, surprise, surprise, a pioneer of *radio* educational broadcasts.

The last word on telly though should go to Desmond King-Hele, a British physicist, author and very brainy man. In 1970 he predicted that by the 1990s we would have, 'three dimensional colour television'. Now if he'd stopped there, he would have done brilliantly. 3D TV is of course a reality as is 3D cinema and both have given broadcasters the right to charge even more for their services. But Mr King-Hele then claimed these pictures would have: '... smell, touch and taste added.'

What he was actually talking about was 4D television which has again come to pass, but this form of entertainment is usually reserved for theme parks and interactive museum displays, where smells of chocolate are pumped into the audience or a rain simulator chucks down showers on spectators.

However, King-Hele was referring to techniques that would be available *for the masses* and in that respect he was wrong. 4D television is not yet a commercial reality, with the possible exception of very wealthy people who might employ a member of staff to spray perfume on them during an advert for a perfume they find particularly appealing. As for the rest of us, a lack of 4D TV is possibly a good thing. After all, with the amount of chemical additives contained in some foodstuffs, tasting it during advert breaks might well lead to food poisoning or possibly choking, in which case a virtual doctor would need to leap out of the screen and perform the Heimlich manoeuvre on you. 2D, non-smelly, tasty or touchy telly really isn't such a bad thing if viewed through that particular prism.

7. Writing the wrongs

When speaking of writing, no less an authority than Socrates made the following prediction.

> ... this discovery ... will create forgetfulness in learners' souls, because they will not use their memories; they will trust to the external written characters and not remember of themselves.

Good job that someone chose to write his words down otherwise they would probably have been forgotten.

Socrates's prediction was quite possibly the first to be made about writing, but by golly, gosh and crikey it wasn't the last; the publishing world is littered with sparkling gems of forecasting fallacy, mainly in the form of rejections that predict abject failure for a manuscript, but for some strange reason always end by wishing the writer all the best for their future career.

Stephen King, that doyen of American sci-fi/fantasy/bloody weird books, kept all his rejection letters on a spike on the headboard of his bed. When he submitted *Carrie* in the hope of securing a first book deal and escaping from his tough teaching job, he received this missive from one publisher:

> We are not interested in science fiction which deals with negative utopias. They do not sell.

Firstly, it's debatable that *Carrie* is about a negative utopia. Negative, yes. Utopia, hmm. Secondly, the prediction about that type of science fiction not selling. Seems odd that the publisher in question hadn't heard of *Brave New World, Animal Farm, 1984, A Clockwork Orange* and other classics that deal with worlds you'd be hard pushed to describe as positive.

Talking of *Animal Farm*, when submitting his devastating critique on totalitarianism George Orwell received the following brush off:

> It is impossible to sell animal stories in the USA.

In this case, there is a chance that this respondent meant it's impossible to sell stories *to* animals in the USA on account of the fact that they have never shown much in the way of reading prowess, failing to master even the most basic of phonetic knowledge. Whatever the case, in years to come, this turner-downer was left looking like a right pig's ear.

Catch-22 by Joseph Heller also received an equally firm put down:

> I haven't really the foggiest idea about what the man is trying to say. .... Apparently the author intends it to be funny – possibly even satire – but it is really not funny on any intellectual level.

Maybe it was funny on a *non*-intellectual level, or maybe the person issuing this biting critique wouldn't recognise humour if it walloped him in the face. Either way Heller had the last laugh.

Someone else who failed to see any merit in a novel that was sent to him was the publisher who, on receiving a copy of *Lord of the Flies* by Mr William Golding, concluded that it was,

> An absurd and uninteresting fantasy which was rubbish and dull.

There most certainly were flies on him.

8. Going for a song

Music and leisure go together like Peters and Lee. Or, for the younger generation, like Lady and Gaga.

The potential for music to relax and entertain probably came about the moment the first ever note was heard, which could well have been the moment a caveman blew into a blowpipe and, quite by chance, played the opening melody of 'Take Me Home Country Road'. Since then a vast industry has grown up in which opinions are given both willy and nilly, and decisions are made in similar fashion.

Most will know and delight in Decca's famous prediction after hearing the Beatles that, '*Guitar bands are on their way out,*' but the tradition of woeful prophecy in the musical arts has a long and ignoble history.

An early shining example of this came from a German composer called Moritz Hauptmann in 1871:

> I do not believe that a single one of Wagner's compositions will live after him.

If Moritz was talking about Brian Wagner, a Bavarian tailor of no musical ability, he was spot on. If he was talking about Richard Wagner, the great composer and conductor, he was spot off. Perhaps if he'd substituted his own name for that of Wagner's his prediction would have been more accurate.

Curiously enough our anarchist art critic friend Herbert Read also mentioned Wagner in that 1964 *New Scientist* article of his.

> The lighter forms of opera will survive (into 1984) because they are entertaining but composers like Beethoven, Wagner and Stravinsky will be forgotten.

Herbie rides again eh, and just as incorrectly.

Of course 'popular music' predictors have screwed up just like their classical counterparts. *Musical America*'s 1957 take on rock-and-roll was that it was merely:

> A passing fad.

Perhaps, but some 55 years later it is still passing and may continue to do so for some considerable time yet.

Back with the Beatles, and if Decca Records can find any comfort in the fact that they turned down the biggest band of all time, it is that others were similarly dismissive of the Fab Four.

> They are a passing phase.

So said Christian evangelist Billy Graham in 1964, possibly

borrowing from *Musical America*'s prediction, though at least limiting it to one act rather than the whole genre. Another who spectacularly failed to see the potential in Liverpool's finest was president of the Beatles American label Capitol Records, Alan Livingston. After turning down, 'Love Me Do', 'Please Please Me' and 'From Me To You,' for American release, he sent a memo to EMI, their parent company in Britain, which read:

We don't think the Beatles will do anything in this market.

Mind you, Alan was in good company because prior to the Beatles' first American tour in 1964, Paul McCartney speculated about whether or not this jaunt was going to be successful:

They've got their own groups. What are we going to give them that they don't already have?

As the Beatles' plane landed in America and the mop-topped lads looked out to see hordes of screaming girls being pinned back by police officers, it must have crossed McCartney's mind that he'd ever so slightly underestimated the band's chances of Stateside success.

HEALTH AND THE HUMAN BODY

They say that two heads are better than one, but for the most part, they mean it figuratively. However, at some point in the future we may all quite literally have two heads.

Now, leaving aside for one moment the implications that would have for childbirth and how the female body would have to change to accommodate such a phenomenon, this non-sensical prediction is actually not so nonsensical when run up against the pantheon of genuine predictions that have been made about our bodies and what the future might hold for them.

We can see *why* some people are so keen to get a hold on the medical future. Humans, for the most part, want to live as long and as healthily as possible (or at least get in a couple of extra shags before they die). Death is not an audition; there's no call back. So predictors in this field have really gone out on a limb, shaping a rosy future where joints don't age, hips don't go on package holidays and bunions are kept at bay. Hundreds of researchers, scientists and doctors have made pin-sharp forecasts that have not only borne fruit but have also come true. This has had huge implications for treatment planning and medication development. Well done those brainy pharmacological types.

Thankfully, there's another branch of health/medical predictors whose predictions never made it to the double doors of the operating theatre. It seems that many of these failed fore-casts develop from a deep-rooted dissatisfaction with the human form. It's almost as if, ever since we made that final leap from being homo erectus to being homo sapiens, or, translating (incorrectly) from the Latin, from monkeys to humans, some people have been distinctly ungrateful with the body that evolution spent millions of years preparing for us. It's mean and spiteful to be sure, but then being mean and spiteful are human traits so they must have some evolutionary benefits of their own. Perhaps they serve to mark out the lunatics who make absurd predictions about our bodies so we can avoid them and live more enjoyable lives.

At some point in the future though, the compulsion to make wildly inaccurate predictions about the human body could well be a treatable condition; doctors might be able to pinpoint the exact area of the brain responsible for this terrible affliction and send in nano-submarines to destroy it. Alternatively, a simple pill might rid the world of this horrendous plague.

That said, the prediction that doctors might be able to treat the compulsion to make predictions about the body, might itself be a ridiculous prediction about the future of healthcare, something which could also be treated by medical practitioners in the future – but only if the prediction that it will be possible to cure people of making ridiculous predictions about the future of healthcare is not a ridiculous assertion itself.

All told, the chances of people not making unbelievable predictions about health and the human body are minimal because they've been doing it for years without the remotest sign of a cure.

1. People will live to be 150. No 50. No, wait a minute, 200. Actually, make that 969. Oh all right then, 42

It doesn't take a genius to figure out that, as a general rule, we, the human race, are getting better at not dying so young. In actual fact we're pretty good at it. In 1900 life expectancy in Europe was about 47, rising to 66 in 1950 and a whopping 73 in 2000, unless you live in Albania in which case it's about 12.

However, something else we're pretty good at is making ludicrous predictions of how long we're all going to live, which would quite probably make the people who made them want to die of embarrassment if they were still around today, thus, ironically, lowering the average and making their predictions even worse.

First out of the traps is the marvellously named Reverend Thomas De Witt Talmage who in 1893 was one of a number of 'notable' Americans asked by the American Press Association to write an article predicting life in the 1990s.

> What American now living will be the most honored by 1993? he posited before adding, 'By that time longevity will be so improved that 150 years will be no unusual age to reach.'

Indeed, though only in dog years. The Reverend's prediction seems to be based on, well, nothing really, though earlier in the article he does say, *'cancer and consumption will be as easily cured as influenza or a 'run round'* (which apparently was diarrhoea), so it would seem he's basing it on better healthcare. But given that we still can't cure influenza today, his knowledge of such was scant to say the least.

A few years later and the pendulum appeared to have swung the other way when, in December 1900, the following prediction about life in the year 2000 appeared in the *Ladies Home Journal*.

> The American will be taller by from one to two inches. His increase of stature will result from better health, due to vast reforms in medicine, sanitation, food and athletics. He will live fifty years instead of thirty-five as at present – for he will reside in the suburbs.

The article, a classic of its genre – it contains numerous gems – was written by a John Elfreth Watkins Jr who points out that,

> To the wisest and most careful men in our greatest institutions of science and learning I have gone, asking each in his turn to forecast for me what, in his opinion, will have been wrought in his own field of investigation before the dawn of 2001 – a century from now. These opinions I have carefully transcribed.

So, therein lies a clue as to what must have happened. Either when it came to life expectancy the person consulted wasn't quite as wise as John Jr imagined or, when it came to transcribing, John Jr wasn't as careful as he thought he was. Or, quite possibly, both. Then again, John Jr may have been well into his late twenties by the time he wrote the article and suffering from the afflictions that such a ripe old age brings.

Fifty though, is a wonderfully conservative prediction of life expectancy, though do bear in mind this is because '*man will reside in the suburbs*'. Clearly 'commuting during the rush hour' was beyond the forecasting skills of the wisest and most careful men of the time because if it had been one feels they would have included it in their calculations and predicted a life expectancy of about 30.

So, the battle lines were drawn between Reverend Thomas De Witt Talmage and John Elfreth Watkins Jr (there's a contest to conjure with). Who would emerge triumphant with the most popular, least accurate prediction?

Well, with the good Lord on his side, it was the Reverend whose influence can clearly be seen in the following two articles. Firstly, there was *The Chicago Daily Tribune* which, in 1925, reported '*75 to be noon of life in year 2000*'. They went on to add that 112½ would be the six o'clock in the evening of life in 2000 and 132¾ would be about 9:15 (way past the bedtime of someone that old).

Then in 1926 came an even more audacious prediction from *The Charleston Gazette*.

A serious scientist has glad news for all those that want to stick to this world, in spite of its troubles and worries. In the year 2000, says he, the average life will be 100 years, and many will live to be 200 years old.

Great stuff, though one wonders what a not-so-serious scientist might have come up with. Interesting also to note that this prediction was made with people who want to 'stick to this world' in mind. Presumably a prediction for those who 'don't want to stick to this world' would be along the lines of 'cyanide pills, rope and the location of hazardous cliff edges will be freely available in the year 2000'.

So 200, 200, any advance on 200? Oh Lordy Lord yes. In 1934 in an article entitled, 'Looking Forward', Thomas Midgley Jr went for broke.

The next century should see an extension in the conquest of science over the forces of nature so astounding that imagination is inadequate to conceive of the final result. Our knowledge of the vital chemical processes of living matter will be so enormously increased that it is not too much to say that the life cycle itself may be controlled to the end that old age shall have disappeared and that many then alive may live to ages rivaling that of Methuselah.

Well, Mr Midgley Jr has certainly stuck his neck out there, along with the rest of his torso, because it's generally agreed that Methuselah lived to be 969, assuming that he was talking about the biblical Methuselah and not, Mr Methuselah Jenkins from Daventry who died at the age of 67. It's a bold prediction indeed, but of course there's a very thin line between bold and brainless and this one skirts that divide precariously.

But a little delving into the mysterious Mr Midgley gives some insight into just why he might have been moved to be so optimistic about the future of the human race. Environmental historian J.R. McNeill has said that Thomas Midgley Jr, 'had more impact on the (earth's) atmosphere than any other single organism in the earth's history'. Another bold claim, but one based on the fact that Thomas Midgley Jr was a mechanical engineer and chemist whose contribution to the world was the development of leaded petrol and CFC gases. Now there's a claim to fame, rivalled only perhaps by Einstein's invention of the atom bomb (in theory at any rate).

Clearly on some level Thomas knew the devastation that would be caused by his creations, so much so that the terrible guilt he felt led to an insane level of denial and thus a fanatically positive prediction of, quite literally, biblical proportions.

Twenty-one years later, in 1955, and *The Charleston Gazette* refused to bow to Midgely pressure; in fact they hadn't changed their opinion much at all. Local doctor Lowry H. McDaniel, they reported, predicted that in 1999, *'a man ninety years old will be considered young, a man of 135 more mature ...'* Great news for the male of the species, but the doctor had even better news for the females. *'Our women,'* he opined, *'thanks to proper hormone medication, would stay young, beautiful and shapely indefinitely.'*

Obviously that's a completely ridiculous prediction. What he should have said was, 'Thanks to plastic surgery our women will stay young, beautiful and shapely forever.'

So, a doctor, a couple of scientists and a man of the cloth all reckoned we would live to far riper and far older ages, whereas in fact, it was their predictions that were destined for longevity and not us.

In 1970, however, sobriety had overtaken those four life-length enhancers and the following was forecast.

By 1980 the life expectancy of all Americans will be 42 years.

This prediction was made at the first Earth Day by one Paul Ehrlich (at last someone with a reasonably sensible name). It was based on fears about air pollution and, clearly, was wrong. Okay, very wrong, especially for any Americans aged 33 or over at the time (work it out). But, annoyingly, Paul's prediction, and others made at the same Earth Day, have been latched on to by some people as examples of why we shouldn't listen to scientists today when they predict global warming disasters and such like. Strangely though, all of those detractors are descendants of people who didn't believe the earth was round.

Clearly then predicting life expectancy is not easy and leaves those who attempt it open to ridicule and humiliation, though mainly by 21st century writers. However, all that could have been avoided if they'd read an article in the May 1938 edition of *Modern Mechanix* under the headline: '*YOUR SHOULDER BLADES PREDICT HOW OLD YOU'LL BE.*' Of course, sometimes the obvious answer is staring you in the face all along and you just don't see it.

This important discovery was made by Dr William Washington Graves who claimed that,

> ... persons having the convex-type of shoulder blades have a better chance in life than those who have straight or concave scapulae, and, 'those with a mixed combination of blade fare more poorly in life than the ones who have both blades either convex or concave.'

Incredibly a Nobel Prize wasn't forthcoming, however Dr Graves did receive a Certificate Of Merit for his work from the St Louis Medical Society, something reported as being an '*outstanding event*', by a popular magazine of the day, *The Eugenics Review*. Oh dear.

2. Old age rejuvenator centrifuge

Living longer is all good and well, but there's not much point if we're going to spend those precious extra years (nigh on 900 of them if Thomas Midgely Jr is to be believed) suffering from incontinence, senility, uncontrolled flatulence and other ravages of old age.

Step forward then the Old Age Rejuvenator Centrifuge as reported in the August 1935 edition of *Modern Mechanix* magazine. The theory behind this startling prediction is that, '*old age, then, is in part a gradual succumbing to the force of gravity*', something illustrated by the following highly complex medical diagram.

Essentially the point being depicted here is that we all get a bit saggy in our latter years, so what's to be done?

We suggest periods of centrifugalization. An individual in special need of treatment might rest at night upon a large revolving disc with his head toward the outer rim; the disc should be so bevelled as to carry the head at a lower level than the feet; optimum (best) speed to be determined by laboratory experimentation. Such a disc might be large enough to carry ten or twenty patients. This mechanism would facilitate the functions which during the day are inhibited by gravity.

So it's a roundabout for bedridden pensioners as imagined in the following illustration.

The mind boggles, and not just because it's revolving at some speed. It's akin to sleeping in a spin dryer, something which, as most cats will testify to, does little for the health, though there may be benefits if the old person does in fact suffer from incontinence. (Perhaps it should be renamed the Sheet Rejuvenator Centrifuge.)

Side effects may include dizziness and sickness, which can be cured by spending all day in a stationary bed.

Having turned full circle during the night, many times, the prediction then itself comes full circle by showing us exactly what the effects of the OARC will be.

Yes, the effects of gravity have been reversed and the man has been 'de-sagged'.

Incredibly the OARC never saw the light of day, or the dark of night, bringing those who predicted its effects down to earth with quite a bump ... because of gravity, do you see?

3. Man of future to have one eye

Suggested in 1934, you could be forgiven for thinking that this prediction was made by a down-on-his-luck monocle manufacturer. Nothing, though, could be further from the truth. It was in fact made by respected eye specialist Dr Thomas Shastid of Minnesota, who, we are told, was also the editor of many optical magazines. Note, if you will, that he is an *eye* specialist and not an *eyes* specialist.

> Man's eyes will come closer and closer together, the bridge of the nose will further diminish, and finally the two eyes will again become one; just one large, Cyclopean eye in the center of the face.

What intrigues here is the notion that, two eyes will *again* become one, implying it would seem, that we are all descended from one-eyed creatures, the evidence for which is wholly underwhelming. In short, there is none, other than in mythology, which isn't really all that scientific. Indeed, there isn't any creature that is known to have just the one organ of vision, so the doctor's prediction does seem to have been a little short-sighted (wahey!) leading many to believe that he himself had just the one brain cell.

Thankfully, it would seem he realised the error of his ways and kept quiet about his other predictions that in the future we would have only one ear, one leg and one breast.

4. In the next 50 years we will evolve into Homo Aquaticus, human fish who will be able to live underwater

This delightful curiosity is the work of none other than famed underwater explorer Jacques Cousteau who made the prediction at the World Congress of Underwater Activities (Towels Provided) in London in 1962. Incredibly, he didn't do it for a bet, he was deadly serious.

> We are now moving toward an alteration of human anatomy, to give man almost unlimited freedom underwater. ... Surgery will affix a set of artificial gills to man's circulatory system which will permit him to breathe oxygen from the water like a fish. Then the lungs will be by-passed and he will be able to live and breathe in any depth for any amount of time without harm. ...

Many suspect that Jacques' main aim in making this prediction was to save money on expensive scuba diving gear and mini-submarines, which can be pricey even when bought second-hand.

His vision though, wasn't simply that human beings would be able to swim with the fishes, in the non-mafia sense.

> Do you realize what that will mean? He will be able to observe, train, cultivate, and exploit the seas at first-hand. Maybe the first man will be an undersea farmer. ...

Now there's a glorious image, an undersea farmer rounding up herds of walrus with his sheep-lobster and chewing on an ear of seaweed.

But Jacques was bold and finished by committing the cardinal sin of predictions, '*it will happen,*' he said. '*I promise you.*' Yes, and pigs might swim.

To be fair to Jacques though, he can probably get away with

one slip up in an otherwise glittering career. Perhaps he was hoping that the transformation to Homo Aquaticus would be based on goldfish and, along with the ability to remain underwater, one would also have a two second memory, in which case his absurd prediction would have been long forgotten. No such luck.

5. Amplified Man

Just when you thought men couldn't get any more amplified, along comes this wonderful contraption that never was – the man-amplifier. It made its strangely subdued appearance in the 1966 book, *Bionics: Nature's Ways For Man's Machines* by Robert Wells, which peaked at number 4,912,319 on the bestsellers list.

> This Man-Amplifier helps the pilot or astronaut encumbered by a clumsy and tiring space suit. Strapped to the man, it is a metal skeleton with electrical motors at important joints. These motors follow the man's body movements, operating when he moves, stopping when he stops – thereby lending greater strength to his muscles.

On one level Robert probably thinks he's been quite clever here. He's looked into the future, to a time when many people will be wearing space suits, and has pre-invented something that he hopes will make a killing.

However, what beggars belief is the notion that the way to un-encumber someone encumbered in quite an awkward outfit is to slap a metal skeleton on top of the suit that is encumbering them and then add electric motors to that. Any sane individual can see that what has been created there is the most encumbering outfit in the universe.

What's more, if you can find the man hidden somewhere beneath all those layers, the chances of him being in any way amplified are nil. On the contrary, he'll probably end up being trapped in there for days because no one was able to hear his shouts for help.

6. Women of the future won't be any more intelligent, in fact, they'll probably be less intelligent

From the 18 March 1911 edition of *London's Penny Illustrated Paper* comes the following from J.C. Bristow-Noble.

> ... rise please from your tomb a hundred years hence and perhaps you will be astounded to find woman not a jot cleverer than her great-grandmother was. Indeed, she will not have the amount of brains that the present day woman can boast.

It's unclear whether J.C. was a man or a woman, but one strongly suspects the former to be the case and that he was attempting to get a job on the *Daily Mail*. It seems that J.C. was driven to his conclusion by the ridiculous notions of, among others, George Bernard Shaw, who outrageously suggested that women would one day eschew the skirt and the petticoat in favour of the tight (sic).

One can see now quite why J.C. was so riled that he felt he

had to illuminate the readers as to the true nature of women-folk, and, rather than simply make the prediction, J.C. also explained the detailed scientific reasoning behind it. *'A woman is a woman'*, he says. *'And try as she may she cannot escape from herself'*.

Unquestionably this fellow was a leading authority on the fairer sex who, should he rise from his tomb in 2011, would find that his prophetic words were spot on, though only if his tomb happened to be in Kerry Katona's bedroom. If he ended up in the labs of any of the world's top female scientists, doctors or professors he might well find himself being experimented on for his ever so slightly prejudiced views.

Mr Bristow-Noble was also not shy of offering other gold nuggets of advice in his article and went on to expound that,

> Any man ... can and always will have the power to make his wife happy if he will only dress her well, feed her daintily and love her perpetually, adding that, 'the life of the badly dressed woman must be unbearable.'

J.C. Bristow-Noble had struck a blow in the battle of the sexes, and one from which it's unlikely men would ever recover. As for the notion of feeding one's wife 'daintily' this would imply that future sales of elegant china teaspoons and delicate finger foods would soar.

7. Intelligence pill

There are many flaws in Mr Bristow-Noble's prediction that women would be less intelligent in 2011 than they were in 1911, but one of the less obvious is his inability to foresee the creation of a pill that would make everyone very intelligent, even women.

It didn't escape James R. Berry though, who, in a 1968 article entitled 'What Will Life Be Like in 2008?', used his somewhat limited intelligence to make just such a prediction.

> No need to worry about failing memory or intelligence either. The intelligence pill is another 21st century commodity. Slow learners or people struck with forgetfulness are given pills which increase the production of enzymes controlling production of the chemicals known to control learning and memory. Everyone is able to use his full mental potential.

It's such a lovely thought. Think of the hours that could be saved by the myriad of people who perpetually lose things. No longer would they have to search high and low for the item; they'd simply pop an intelligence pill and suddenly remember where they left it, which would, of course, be in the last place they were going to look.

That in itself could lead to problems though. Particularly forgetful people might end up overdosing and creating a master race of super-intelligent beings. What if the Stephens Fry and Hawking took a pill? Would their heads explode and increase their production of award-winning documentaries to one per second?

Ultimately though, we should all rejoice in the fact that this prediction was way off the mark for the simple (not intelligent) reason that a world without stupid people is a pretty dull place. Just think, there'd be no *Jeremy Kyle Show*, footballers would give thought-provoking interviews, and George W. Bush wouldn't have kept us in hysterics by saying all those moronic things.

The greatest irony though is that if such a pill had existed, the chances are that James R. Berry would have swallowed one and therefore been unable to make such an idiotic prediction.

8. Space hospitals

The American Rocket Society has reported to President Eisenhower that practical medical science could benefit importantly from the weightlessness, irradiation and low temperatures of outer space. So we may find that some of tomorrow's hospitals may actually be anchored in the heavens.

These are the words of legendary futurist illustrator Arthur Radebaugh who produced the 'Closer Than You Think' comic strip, which was syndicated to Sunday papers in America from 1958–62.

The above prediction was one of his earliest, appearing in 1958, and it cannot have escaped your attention that while the strip is called, 'Closer Than You Think', the hospitals in this instance are a lot further away than you, or anyone for that matter, ever thought. Getting to them would clearly be rather difficult, unless you had your own personal spaceship, and the emergency services would surely be struggling.

'Hello? I think I'm having a heart attack.'

'Okay, we can have a space ambulance with you in about 36 hours.'

'36 hours!? Can't you get here any sooner?'

'Sir, I assure you that that is a very rapid response time. The ambulance has to prepare for take off, then re-enter the earth's orbit before splash landing at sea from where it'll be picked up and taken to dry land. It will then make its way to you with great haste. Have a good day.'

Similarly, visiting someone in the hospital would prove challenging. 'I'm just going to see how Dad's recovering from his hip replacement, back in four days.'

Weightlessness would also be an issue, though incredibly Arthur goes on to suggest it could be an advantage.

One of these hospitals might be shaped like a disc atop elevator tubes leading to the control section. The mushroom-like disc would contain weightless operating rooms for treating heart and other organic troubles as well as bone diseases.

Weightless operating rooms? It's tough enough performing surgery with full gravity, how hard is it going to be while afloat? There'd be blood and body parts everywhere with nurses ducking to avoid scalpels.

'The operation went well madam and we successfully removed your appendix. There was a slight complication though, unfortunately one of your kidneys was sucked into a black hole.'

It seems unlikely that we'll see hospitals anchored in the heavens any time soon, though when we do no doubt there'll be an Arthur Radebaugh wing, or ideally two to keep it well balanced up there.

9. Human beings of the future will become one-toed

This prediction was made in a lecture to The Royal College of Surgeons of England in 1911 by one Richard Clement Lucas. Having mercilessly slagged off the little toe, Mr Lucas proceeded thus:

> On the other hand the great toe has undergone extraordinary development because the inner side of the foot is the first to catch the centre of gravity in transferring the weight of the body from one foot to the other in walking and I ventured to predict that if the world went on long enough, in perhaps half a million years as the useless outer toes being less and less employed gradually disappeared, man might become a one-toed race.

Clearly Mr Lucas had never enjoyed the thrill of having his tootsies partake in a round of 'this little piggy went to market', for if he had, he would have known not to suggest such a ridiculous notion. How on earth is the little piggy to go 'wee wee wee' all the way home, let alone have any roast beef, with just the one toe?

That aside, his prediction is the work of a very prejudiced man, an example of early 20th century toe-ism. Toe lovers of today would be up in arms with his categorisation of the four smaller digits as the 'useless outer toes', and his obvious bias towards the big toe. Great toe indeed.

10. The Tooth Bank

Squint for a moment into the crystal ball labeled 'Dental Science's Coming Attractions.'

So begins a 1947 article from *Modern Mechanix* magazine under the heading, 'How About Tooth Banks?'

As catchy opening sentences go it's not up there with the most enticing and leads to two thoughts; 'no thanks', and, 'if I have to squint, shouldn't I be looking into the crystal ball labelled *Optical* Science's Coming Attractions?'

Nonetheless, it's worth persevering with the article, getting your teeth into it if you will, because the prediction is that much in the same way that people donate blood, at some point in the future they'll be able to donate teeth. These donor teeth can then be transplanted into a patient's mouth where they will fuse with the gums and take their rightful place alongside the other 31 (assuming that person is just having the one transplant . . .).

It's a great idea, but, as with many great ideas there is one teensy weensy negligible barely worth mentioning flaw. Conveniently, blood replenishes itself, inconveniently, grown-up teeth do not, such that if an adult was to deposit a tooth in the bank, they would have to withdraw it themselves, in which case they'd need to replace it, which makes it hardly worth donating it in the first place, especially as it's unlikely to have accrued any interest during the time it was in the bank.

Overlooking this minor point the article continues in optimistic vein.

> They (Scientists) are convinced that eventually they will succeed, and with success will come one of the greatest boons to mankind. Picture the possibilities: Into the junkpile will go all artificial dentures, all bridges, plates, partial plates. All men and women of whatever age will be able to have human teeth imbedded inside their gums until the day they die.

One of the greatest boons to mankind? Well then, let's divert all the funding that goes to finding a cure for cancer and battling heart disease to ensuring we all have a cracking set of gnashers by the time we cop it.

For the time being 'biting into an apple at the age of 90' will have to be relegated down the list of science's priorities, probably to just below the battle to defeat the scourge of splinters.

As for the crystal ball marked, 'Dental Science's Coming Attractions', it's been deposited in the Crystal Ball bank, otherwise known as the Dustbin of Discarded Floss.

11. By 1975 we'll have no teeth

From a wealth of teeth to an absence of them completely – another example of how extreme this predictive business can be. If only the folk attempting to set up those tooth banks had bothered to pick up a copy of the *Brooklyn Daily Eagle* back in 1900, they'd have known not to waste their time because there, in black and white was the following prediction:

> Teeth will disappear in about 75 years from now, because the food of the future will be concentrated and made directly from chemicals so that there will be no strain on the digestion, or gums.

It was made by C.M. Skinner, and, tempting as it is to presume that the C.M. stands for Completely Mad, he was a respected journalist, right up to the time that his thoughts on teeth were published.

Of course, it's not just the demise of teeth that he's predicting, but the end of proper food, farming, biting and, most devastatingly of all, pooing, which, more than anything, should have alerted him to the error of his ways.

Indeed, given that a goodly many gentlemen of the time probably took to the lavatory with a copy of the *Brooklyn Daily Eagle*, and a pipe, had Mr Skinner been correct in his assertion, many of his readers would have been deprived of their combined reading/pooing pleasure, an unthinkable state of affairs and one that has almost certainly done more to hold back the development of chemical foodstuffs than any other.

12. Can frozen sleep cure cancer?

In a word, no. However, this was one of the predictions made in *Popular Science* magazine based on an experiment into suspended animation performed by two doctors in the 1930s. The experiment was carried out at the Temple University Hospital in Philadelphia, and given that one of the medics was called Dr *Temple* S. Fay, therein may lie a little clue as to how he was able to get the go-ahead for instructing 32 women suffering from cancer to strip naked and, '*be packed in ice like frozen fish*'. As fetishes go, that is way, way out there.

The women were kept in their frozen state for no less than five days whereupon they were awoken with '*hot applications and steaming coffee*'. Presumably both were thrown over them for the purposes of defrosting.

Results were apparently very positive, with improvements being made to most of the patients ... before they died.

Incredibly, a film was made of the entire procedure, which is available from specialist web sites and some fishmongers.

Those in the medical community who were shown the film were very excited by it, so much so that some of them even asked for their own personal copies that they could study more fully in the privacy of their own homes.

In actual fact, freezing cancer cells *is* currently being looked into, and Doctor Temple S. Fay may have been onto something. However, for some strange reason, today's researchers aren't confining their studies to naked women.

As for any follow up research to this experiment, in the 1930s, *Popular Science* notes that,

> After the sensation created by the announcement of their first successes, they have drawn a protective veil of secrecy about their experiments, while they pursue their extraordinary line of research.

One can only hazard a guess at what went on behind that veil.

13. Stupid surgeons

Surgeons are generally held in high regard, unlike sturgeons, which are not, other than perhaps by lovers of caviar. As cutter-uppers of the human body it's probably as well that they are so revered, particularly by their patients, though from time to time they do seem to go out of their way to knock themselves from their esteemed perches (not the fish).

One such example came about in 1839 when the famous French anatomist and surgeon Alfred Velpeau made the following prediction:

> The abolishment of pain in surgery is a chimera. It is absurd to go on seeking it today. 'Knife' and 'pain' are two words in surgery that must forever be associated in the consciousness of the patient. To this compulsory combination we shall have to adjust ourselves.

It seems we shall also have to adjust ourselves to the fact that the words 'sadistic' and 'bastard' were forever in the consciousness of Mr Velpeau, or to give him his full name, Alfred Armand Louis Marie Velpeau (yes, there's a girl's name in there).

It's a shame Al made that prediction when he did though, because had he waited a few short years later, until anaesthetics, ether and chloroform made their appearance in the world of medicine, he could have saved himself an awful lot of embarrassment.

A short hop across the Channel and 34 years into the future and another leading light of the surgery establishment was staking his claim to be the absurdist medical forecaster of the millennium. Sir John Erichsen is thought of as one of the fathers of modern surgery. He was president of The Royal College of Surgeons and surgeon-extraordinary to Queen Victoria, so perhaps he was trying to amuse the old dear when he came out with this assertion:

> There cannot always be fresh fields of conquest by the knife; there must be portions of the human frame that will ever remain sacred from its intrusions, at least in the surgeon's hands. That we have already, if not quite, reached these final limits, there can be little question. The abdomen, the chest, and the brain will be forever shut from the intrusion of the wise and humane surgeon.

Thank goodness then for stupid and inhumane surgeons who saw fit to ignore Sir John and decided on balance that his vision wasn't really brain surgery.

WORK AND THE WORKPLACE

Obviously when it comes to work, the only prediction anyone is really interested in hearing is, 'you will win the lottery tomorrow and never have to work again'. Unfortunately that outcome befalls a minuscule proportion of the world's population. For the most part adults *need* to work so they can pay for a bus ticket to their workplace, where they can earn enough money to pay for a bus ticket home.

Faced with the reality of having to labour, many people turn to the phrase 'work/life balance' in the hope that this particular split outlined in their working contract may be 1 per cent to 99 per cent. After all, if work isn't part of your life, it's your anti-life and so should be minimised wherever possible. Sadly though, contractual emphasis is usually the other way around and apparently at Walmart, the *life* side of things can go into negative numbers.

But there's always hope and those working in the field of work-related predictions are often spurred on by the possibility that in the future we'll be able to work shorter hours for more money and greater leisure time. How about the 80-minute toilet break, or the three-hour lunch anyone?

But how could such a radical change in the work/life

equation ever be achieved? Workplace sabotage is one option, hiding is another but more realistic is increased mechanisation. Some view the further encroachment of machines in the workplace as a threat, while others see it as a boon; maybe one day, every single job will be carried out by some sort of contraption, allowing humans to boss the contraptions around in the name of performing a 'management' role.

But as all of the work-related predictors in this chapter get things so wrong, it would seem that increased mechanisation in *their field* might well be the answer as A) it might result in more accurate predictions and B) it would force them to get a proper job.

1. Working nine to one. Or twelve. Or eleven

The main obsession with those who have sought to delve into the future of our working lives seems to be just how much less time we're all going to be toiling away thanks to the many wonderful technological innovations that are sure to have been invented in order to do most of the work for us.

Yes, well, there have indeed been a fair few innovations, but as we all know the only reason we might be spending less time trying to earn a living today is because we're so over-worked and knackered that we keep having to throw sickies.

A research study by the European Foundation for the Improvement of Living and Working Conditions reported in 2008 that on average in the United Kingdom people work 41.4 hours a week. Granted, 41 of those hours might involve checking their emails, but they're still technically 'at work'.

That might come as something of a shock to William Alfred Peffer, a US senator who, in 1893, asserted that, *'In the next century the time of daily toil will be shortened to four or five hours'.* That would be a 20- or 25-hour week, which is not all that radical, but for reasons that shall have to remain a mystery,

Willie then adds another few words explaining how the reduction in daily toil is to be achieved. '*All willing hands will be employed.*'

The implication here is that those unwilling to work will not be employed and it is only through the efforts of the willing that the working day will be shortened.

In that case, with those who didn't want to do anything out of the picture, surely in order to knock off earlier, the willing would have to work twice as hard in less time, which, if not physically impossible, would leave them so utterly exhausted that all they'd be able to do with their extra leisure time would be sleep. Not really worth all that effort is it?

In 1923 an article appeared in a Connecticut newspaper entitled, 'Thinking Men and Women Predict Problems of World Century Hence', one of which might well have been how to write titles for newspaper articles. Within this great work was a section written by an engineer by the name of Walter N. Polakov who, unlike Willie, did opt for the more standard reason as to why we'd be working so little in the future.

Work will gradually become more and more mental and less physical; hours of work that 100 years ago were sixteen per day and today eight, in 2022 will be not over two hours a day because of the advance in technique.

Two hours. Rather than traipsing into work every day and then back home again at the end of those two hours, you might as well do them all in one ten-hour day and have the rest of the week off. Okay, it's not 2022 yet, so Wally might yet prove not to have been quite such a wally, but don't bet on it, particularly as he went on to say this:

Considerable leisure created by highly specialized experts will call for regenerative recreation and play thus compensating for narrow specialization by broadest development of human personalities in all directions without the tint and sting of mercenarism.

It's almost a foreign language. A large number of today's thinking men and women have attempted to decipher it, but to date, none have been successful.

To 1934 now and *The Challenge of Leisure*, a book by author Arthur Newton Pack. It was a time when America was gingerly beginning to come out of its great depression and thus many were looking ahead to happier times and predicting great advances; advances which would, of course, lead to more leisure time. But how would all this time be spent? Arthur reckoned he had some of the answers.

> Just what is this New Leisure then? Manufacturers of cigarettes will tell you that it is time well spent smoking ever greater quantities of cigarettes ... it is time to ... beautify your schoolgirl complexion ... time to invest in guns. ...

In short it seems that it's a time to put on a load of make-up, go and shoot people and give yourself lung cancer. There's a reason to strive for shorter working hours if ever there was three, but just how long could people expect to be spending at their place of employment?

> It would be a rash prophet who denies the possibility that this generation may live to see a two hour day.

And with the onset of this two-hour day, Arthur talks about the need for young people to participate in 'constructive leisure' as opposed to the following sort of frivolity:

> Teach Junior an acceptable activity that will absorb all his interest, and automatically you have removed the danger of his putting

fly-paper on the cat's paws, tinting Mother's frock with jam,
making a football of Father's favourite hat. ...

Compared to what *'Junior'* gets up to today, all three of those
sound like perfectly acceptable activities.

    A couple of years later and with Arthur's prediction showing
no signs of coming to pass, things were modified, though only
very slightly.

By 1960, work will be limited to 3 hours a day.

Thus spake writer John Langdon-Davies in *A Short History of the
Future*, which presumably was short because he only spent three
hours a day working on it. John was still around in the Sixties
and in fact published three books in the early part of the decade,
a remarkable feat given all that leisure time he must have been
having.

    In 1950 so called News Specialists of the Associated Press put
together an article entitled, 'How Experts Think We'll Live In
2000 AD'. (Note that they helpfully added, 'AD' just in case
anyone thought the article might be about 2000 BC.) In the
section headed, 'Labor: A Short Work Week' the readers were
given the following advice:

    ... tell your children not to be surprised if the year 2000 finds a
    35 hour or even a 20 hour work week fixed by law.

Currently the law in the UK states that adults can't be forced
to work more than 48 hours a week, so they were, well, wrong,
something which they might have been better off telling their
children not to be surprised by.

    The notion that children of the 1950s might be surprised by
a shorter working week is in itself fairly preposterous though.
The assumption seems to be that, were it not for the advice
given in the article, it would have suddenly crept up on those

same children, who by then would be over 50, and caught them completely off guard. How terrible would that have been?

If ever there was a time to work less and play more, it was the Swinging Sixties, though for most people that was just a hallucination, probably brought on by working too hard. What were real though, were more predictions about how little we'd all be doing in the future to earn our daily bread.

The programme for the 1962 Century 21 World Fair in Seattle promised:

> We'll work shorter hours. We'll have more time for art, sports and hobbies. ... Executives of the next century will earn a minimum of twelve thousand dollars a year for a twenty-four hour work week.

No doubt no one wanted to be labelled a rash prophet so they all believed every word, whereas the reality today is that a lot of executives in big corporations earn $12,000 a second for doing very little.

In 1967, Pulitzer Prize-winning author Sebastian de Grazia got in on the act and was quoted as having predicted the possibility of a 21-hour working week by the year 2000, dropping to 16 hours 20 years later. For him though the prospect of all that leisure time was the cause for some concern.

> There is reason to fear, as some do, that free time, forced free time, will bring on the restless tick of boredom, idleness, immorality, and increased personal violence. If the cause is identified as automation and the preference for higher intelligence, nonautomated jobs may increase, but they will carry the stigma of stupidity. Men will prefer not to work rather than to accept them. Those who do accept will increasingly come to be a politically inferior class.

Surely the whole point of automation is to do all the menial jobs that no one wants to do, yet here is someone claiming that non automated jobs, presumably non menial, skilled ones, will increase, but anyone who does them will be thought of as an idiot and politically inferior. That doesn't seem to leave any work for anyone who doesn't want to be thought of as a complete moron. Seems pretty clear who is carrying the stigma of stupidity in this situation. Pulitzer Prize, shmulitzer prize.

1968 saw the publication of an article in *Mechanix Illustrated* that went under the heading, '40 Years In The Future'. Naturally it had something to say about work, but there was also a unique take on how we were going to spend some of our newly earned free time.

> People have more time for leisure activities in the year 2008. The average work day is about four hours. But the extra time isn't totally free. The pace of technological advance is such that a certain amount of a jobholder's spare time is used in keeping up with the new developments – on the average, about two hours of home study a day. Most of this study is in the form of programmed TV courses, which can be rented or borrowed from tape libraries.

It's homework basically, but carried over into adult life with the added assumption that there's just no way we'd be able to figure out how to use all this new technology unless we got our heads down for a couple of hours each day.

Thankfully, modern day innovators have taken into account just how thick most of us are and have produced wonderful new inventions such as mobile phones and iPads which a monkey could learn to use in about three minutes (and most humans in about ten).

Fourteen years later and, despite no clear signs of anything changing, Marvin Cetron and Thomas O'Toole raised everyone's hopes yet again in their book, *Encounters With The Future*,

> There will be shorter work weeks, 32 hours a week by 1990 and 25 hours a week by 2000.

So five hours a day by the year 2000; no doubt a youngster reading that in 1982 would have been very excited at the prospect. Clearly though it wasn't going to be all leisure, leisure, leisure come the new millennium, there was still work to be done, but what sort of plum job did Marv and Tommy advise their readers to go for?

> Unless you are the kind of pessimist who thinks robots will build robots to repair robots, you can count on a robot technician's job to be a ticket into the 21st century.

Well, currently the top three most popular jobs in America are, in ascending order, retail salespeople, cashiers and office clerks. Followed by food preparation and service workers, nurses and waiters. Robot technician doesn't make it into the top 15, at which point this particular list ends, which might make a certain kind of pessimist think Marv and Tommy are talking shite.

Oh it might seem a little 'cup half empty', but then elsewhere in the book, we are told the following . . .

> The time is not far off when people will live as long as trees.

. . . which is hardly going to do much to dissuade those in the 'talking shite' camp.

Perhaps rather than predicting less time at work for other people, futurists and their ilk should be the ones spending less time at work, they could certainly do with some time off.

The great irony in all this though is that it's not to the future that we should be looking, but the past. It's pretty much accepted that early hunter-gatherer societies had far more leisure time than we have today. Estimates vary, but it's reckoned that they spent on average about five hours a day doing what constituted work – at a guess, probably hunting and gathering – and sometimes for only a couple of days a week.

It seems then that the way to work less is to grab a spear and spend a few short hours each day hunting bison. So much for technological advances making life easier for everyone.

2. No need to rush hour

With no one being quite rash enough to suggest that by now we'd all be teleporting to work, most past predictors foresaw a future where, whether it was for two hours a day, eight or eighteen, getting to work, and then getting back home again was still going to have to be factored in when considering the future of the daily grind.

In 1950, science writer Waldemar Kaempffert made the following prediction, quite possibly while stuck in a traffic jam on his way to the office.

> In 2000 commuters will go to the city in huge aerial buses that hold 200 passengers. Hundreds of thousands more will make such journeys twice a day in their own helicopters.

What Waldemar seems to have done here is simply transfer the chaos on the roads to the skies. You'd barely be able to move up there for aerial buses and personal helicopters. Before long, no doubt, there'd also be double-decker aerial buses, bendy aerial buses, taxi-copters, police-copters and, of course, illegal immigrants in jet packs offering to clean your windscreen while you were waiting at aerial traffic lights.

The skies would be gridlocked, and as for landing and parking, it doesn't bear thinking about. The sensible commuter would surely think, sod this for a lark and get in the car. With everyone battling their way to work in the air, the roads would be empty and they'd get to the office in no time.

While Waldemar's future might have been almost literally pie in the sky, others who were more grounded still had their heads in the clouds somewhat. Here's what James R. Berry, author of that '40 Years in the Future' article had to say in 1968.

It's 8 a.m., Tuesday, Nov. 18, 2008, and you are headed for a business appointment 300 miles away. You slide into your sleek, two-passenger air-cushion car, press a sequence of buttons and the national traffic computer notes your destination, figures out the current traffic situation and signals your car to slide out of the garage. Hands free, you sit back and begin to read the morning paper, which is flashed on a flat TV screen over the car's dashboard. Tapping a button changes the page. The car accelerates to 150 mph in the city's suburbs, then hits 250 mph in less built-up areas, gliding over the smooth plastic road. ... Traffic is heavy, typically, but there's no need to worry. The traffic computer, which feeds and receives signals to and from all cars in transit between cities, keeps vehicles at least 50 yards apart. There hasn't been an accident since the system was inaugurated.

One hundred and fifty miles an hour! In the suburbs! At about the same time as the school run! There aren't enough exclamation marks in the world to describe the sheer horror! That traffic computer had better be good or there's going to be carnage! On the other hand though, perhaps there wouldn't be any problems; all the kids that get hit would just bounce back up off the plastic road. The driver probably wouldn't notice a thing either, he'd be far too engrossed in the newspaper's sports section.

It's essentially air traffic control for the road programmed by a computer which has the added ability to remotely activate a car's brakes if it gets within 50 yards of another vehicle. All good and well as long as everything else on the road is hooked into it; God help the poor cyclist who happens to have been overlooked by the computer and is taken out at 150 mph as he's pottering happily along one of those suburban roads.

In 1972 Geoffrey Hoyle, son of famed astronomer Sir Fred Hoyle, published a book entitled *2010: Living In The Future*.

Having predicted a three-day working week he then explained the knock on effect that this, and other advances such as vision phones and vision desks, would have when it came to the daily commute.

> With few people travelling to work there are no morning or evening rush hours – no streets crowded with cars, buses and people. Gone are the oily smells and fumes of traffic. When people travel they go by electric car, bus or train.

So there are no streets crowded with cars, buses and people, yet when people travel they use cars, buses and trains. Wouldn't it be just as crowded therefore?

It's a moot point indeed, but then Geoff does something rather odd. He goes back in time from 2010 to the end of the 20th century.

> In 2010 people can live and breathe in clean fresh surroundings, but it was not always like this. At one time late in the twentieth century, millions of people fought their way to school and work every morning. Thick fumes lay over the streets making people cough and cry. There were just too many people trying to get into too small a space all at the same time.

Given that Geoff was writing in 1972 this still counts as a prediction, even though he'd already predicted beyond it, to a time when everything was far more idyllic.

It's hard to know though quite what went on to change things so much in the short time between 'late in the twentieth century' and 2010. Perhaps all those people crying in the streets as they struggled to get to work finally decided enough was enough and staged some sort of environmental revolution.

One thing Geoff could never have anticipated would happen in 2010, however, was the fact that his book would be rediscovered and, thanks to a concerted Facebook campaign, republished as *2011: Living In The Future*, giving many of today's commuters the chance to flick through it as they make their way to work, though only if they're not squashed in too tightly with the millions of others on the train or bus.

3. *The orifice*

At one time the orifice/office gag was considered to have been the very height of hilarity. Who could possibly have foreseen that its use today would mark someone out as being a complete dickhead?

Such is the difficulty inherent in all predictive activity concerning the office with many of those who have considered the future of this most common of workplaces being thought of in similar vein.

Take the BBC's one time flagship science programme *Tomorrow's World* for example. In 1969 presenter James Burke, the name is more than apposite in this instance, starred in a short film to show viewers what it would be like to work in an office of the future. He plays the part of the boss and begins by walking through a relatively busy, open plan office with predominantly women working at their desks. Each is greeted with a breezy 'morning!' before James arrives at his own office, which is a triumph of minimalism. All it contains is a Perspex desk with what, at first glance, appears to be a white sideboard to the right of it.

As the voiceover tells us how quiet, uncluttered and above all, efficient the office is, James sits down and makes a few notes. He then presses a button on his desk to summon what we're told is BJ 39. At this point the white sideboard starts slowly moving around to James's side of the desk. *It* is BJ 39 for goodness' sake, with the BJ probably standing for something sweet and innocent such as Bob a Job and not what many depraved minds of the 21st century might be thinking, although it does make James appear to be a complete cock.

He then tells us:

> BJ 39, much better than a human being. Anything I want, it brings ... even company.

The company in question is a recorded video message on a small television monitor, one of the many fantastic gadgets on BJ 39. (They're not even built into it, they've simply been placed on it.) The others are a camera that looks as if it's from the Victorian era, a tape recorder and a coffee machine.

As James dictates a letter into the tape recorder, the film cuts away to his secretary Miss Smith filing her nails, and the voiceover reminds us how late, inefficient and talkative she was and how often James threatened to fire her. James proudly asserts:

> No more of that nonsense now, I'm an automated executive.

As visions of the future go it's incredibly unadventurous, dull, lacklustre and wrong, though we're never told the exact point in the future that we could expect to see this office. Perhaps there's a clue in the title of the show and they were in fact looking ahead just 24 hours to the following day. Then, the day after that BJ 39 very efficiently finds its way to the scrapheap.

Aside from the addition of various space age gizmos, the other main prediction about offices in the future concerned something they'd have an awful lot less of; paper. The paperless office was first predicted in an article in *Business Week* magazine in 1975.

> Some believe that the paperless office is not that far off. Vincent E. Giuliano of Arthur D. Little, Inc., figures that the use of paper in business for records and correspondence should be declining by 1980, 'and by 1990, most record-handling will be electronic.'

Cut to two trees in the Amazon rainforest looking dolefully at each other and thinking, 'ah, if only'.

Despite the paperless office showing little sign of becoming a reality, the idea itself persisted. In 1993 the *New York Times* quoted Paul Saffo, a consultant at the Institute for the Future as saying,

> In the long run we are going to become paperless in the same way we became horseless. Horses are still around, but they're just ridden by little girls and hobbyists.

These were wise and admirable pronouncements and thousands of businesses around the world have made enormous strides to rid their workplaces of paper trails. There are indeed quite a number of firms that handle all of their records electronically. So top marks to *Business Week* and Mr Paul Saffo. However, sadly for the planet, the facts are that worldwide, the use of paper in offices doubled between 1980 and 2000, and even though there has been a slight decrease since then, as the mountains of A4 reams available in many high street shops will testify to, there's probably more chance of a paper office happening some time soon than there is of a paperless office.

4. All work and no play doesn't bother me, I'm a robot

The promise of all this leisure time in the future wasn't predicated on the fact that there would be any less to do – roads were still going to have to be swept, rubbish was still going to have to be collected and things were still going to have to be assembled on assembly lines – instead it was based on who, or rather, what, was going to be doing it.

The word 'robot' was first used in 1920 and has its root in the Slavic word robota, which means dull, hard work done, more often than not, by someone in servitude. No surprise then that in 1900 when editor of the *Brooklyn Daily Eagle* C.M.

Skinner made a prediction about work in the future, he didn't actually use the term.

> It is hardly necessary to inform you that life [a hundred years hence] will be as nearly a holiday as it is possible to make it. Work will be reduced to a minimum by machinery. Everything will be brought to your hand by deaf and dumb waiters and sliding shelves, operated by electricity supplied to the entire country by the power of the sea.

The misplaced confidence is really quite staggering, though it's also quite touching that our forebears thought we'd have advanced so much as to make life one, big holiday.

Clearly without being able to say as much Mr Skinner is hinting at some form of robot doing most of the work, but what intrigues is the deaf and dumb waiters. The term dumb waiter to refer to a revolving service tray and more latterly a small elevator, has been around for many years, since the 1700s, but no reference exists to anything similar being known as a deaf and dumb waiter. Could it be that he's actually talking about people who are deaf and dumb? The sliding shelves and the fact that he talks about them, and possibly the deaf and dumb waiters, being operated by all this sea-generated electricity, makes it seem unlikely, but in the absence of certainty it's an image worth holding on to. If only he'd suggested that the washing up was going to be done by blind waiters, then we'd know for sure.

In the 1930s, a series of predictions appeared entitled, 'The Age of Power and Wonder', but rather than beguile newspaper readers with their visions of the future, these particular predictions came on cigarette cards in cigarette packets. Perhaps the manufacturers wanted to take their customers' minds off the possibility that if they continued smoking their product they'd only have limited futures themselves.

Card number 225 was enticingly entitled 'Our Future

Servants?' and next to a picture of a robot with surprisingly large ears the smokers of the Thirties were told the following:

> A time is coming when men will no longer need to employ men to do menial work. A great part of industrial work is already being done by machinery, and many experiments have been made in providing domestic mechanical servants. The form they will take has always been imagined rather like this picture, but in fact there is no real reason why they should be like this.

Despite extensive research no record of the reported experiments was found to exist, though that seems unimportant when compared to the fact that they've gone to all the bother of depicting a domestic mechanical servant, only to point out that it might not look anything like the way they have depicted it.

That's no good to anyone, least of all those in the prediction business. It might look like that, it might not. It might happen like that, it might not. It might be invented, it might not. It hardly makes looking ahead to the future the most exact of sciences.

A domestic mechanical servant may look like this

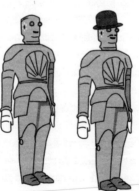

Or it may look like this

A far more precise prediction of how robots were going to replace human workers was made by inventor H. Russell Brand (honestly, that was his name, you couldn't make it up). Until the Thirties, H. Russell's only invention of any note seems to have been some sort of accounting system for shopkeepers, but then he struck, if not gold, then certainly the ears of a few journalists with column inches to fill.

> The machine age is about to take control of the world's largest industry — the $23,000,000,000-a-year restaurant business. Hungry patrons will push various buttons representing items on the menu, their orders will be transmitted electrically to kitchen robots which will prepare their food, deliver it, collect the bills and carry off the dishes.

So reported a newspaper in Ohio about a restaurant Brand proposed to open the following year in New York. Apparently he had all the necessary patents, but at the time of writing only one machine had been invented; an automatic wheat cake cooker and server, which makes him quite possibly the most wildly optimistic person in the entire history of the world.

But wait, we're told that the inventor is in the process of completing his second machine, one that, '*will turn out two poached eggs on toast*'. That's the menu sorted then and as long as you like wheat cakes and poached eggs there's no reason to assume the restaurant will be anything other than a roaring success.

There's still more though. With the success of his restaurant assured, Brand was already looking ahead.

> I already have patents and machines which will cook food and deliver it thru (sic) apartment houses at the pressing of a button. Within five years New York apartment house wives will be able to do all their cooking at a keyboard of these buttons. I am also designing automatic food machines for the Russian government which will be used in community restaurants.

Oh dear, sounds like a case for the Un-American Activities Committee.

Rather brilliantly the article described Brand as, *'the gray-haired, dynamic, carelessly clad inventor'*, which essentially makes him out to be an old, excitable idiot who can't dress himself. Perhaps that was indeed the case because, sadly, a year later, there were no reports of any openings of restaurants staffed entirely by robots.

A slight detour now, away from our mechanical chums, to a somewhat startling prediction about workers of the future made in 1964. That year everyone was getting very excited about the future due to the impressive looking world fair opening on 22 April in New York.

Wandering around among the many mind-bogglingly mind-boggling exhibits was science fiction legend Arthur C. Clarke who was nabbed by a film crew and asked to give his factual thoughts on what the future held. The resulting interview went out later that year on the BBC *Horizon* programme and contained some fascinating insights, in particular this one about how new technology would affect the employment prospects of, in particular, butlers, maids and chauffeurs. Animal lovers look away now.

One of the coming techniques will be what we might call bio-engineering, the development of intelligent and useful servants among the other animals on this planet, particularly the great apes and in the oceans, the dolphins and whales.

In some respects of course this is also a prediction about robot workers, only in this instance, the robots are animals who, as their natural selves in their natural habitats would roam free and live the lives nature intended them to, whereas, according to Clarke the forthcoming great advances would change all that and turn them into slaves for the human race. Now that's progress. Incredibly though Clarke goes on to admonish us for not having done this already.

> You know it's a scandal of which we should be thoroughly ashamed that pre-historic man tamed all the domestic animals we have today, yet we haven't added one in the last five thousand years. It's about time we did so, and with our present knowledge of animal psychology and genetics, we could certainly solve the servant problem with the help of the monkey kingdom.

That servant problem really was terrible back in the Sixties, apparently some members of the aristocracy even had to do without a scullery maid.

It's remarkable that Clarke seems to think the fact that we *haven't* buggered about with the genetic make-up of monkeys, turned them into zombies and put them into domestic service is a reason to be shameful. No wonder he turned down that patronage of the World Wildlife Fund. Wouldn't it be far more humane just to leave a load of monkeys in a room and wait? If they'll eventually write Shakespeare, surely they'll figure out the correct way to serve tea to a duchess.

Once we've got all these simian servants though, it wouldn't all be plain sailing. According to Arthur, things would be okay for a bit, but then we'd be in for a spot of bother.

> ... of course eventually our super chimpanzees would start forming trade unions and we'd be right back where we started. ...

Not entirely sure what he's taking as his starting point here because a society in which militant genetically modified servant chimpanzees are out on strike demanding a minimum wage of four bananas an hour has never, to anyone's knowledge, happened before.

Surely the answer is obvious though. Once the apes get

uppity we just move on to another species who can act as servants to both humans and chimps. Wilderbeest perhaps. Or slugs maybe. Come on Arthur, do try and be a little imaginative with your predictions please.

Having made the world of science fiction a laughing stock when it came to attempting any crossover into science fact, Arthur looked to his colleagues to prove to the world that those of his ilk weren't all mental. Arthur wasn't the only brilliant sci-fi writer that took a long hard look at work and the workplace of the future. Isaac Asimov came out with the following in 1974.

> ... in the 21st century, if we survive, we can imagine that our technological society will advance even further. There will be even more computerization and automation. The dull work of the world will be done by machines. Men and women themselves will be able to do the kind of work they want to do.

Asimov and others writing in a similar vein clearly over-estimated men and women's desire to work at all; the kind of work most men and women want to do is *no* work.

The notion that great armies of robots were just waiting around the next corner to come and relieve us of the burden of work just wouldn't go away though. In 1980 *Newsweek* magazine told its readers that within 20 years robots would replace at least half of all American factory workers and in 1985 author Brian Morris penned *The World of Robots* in which we were told that,

> As city life grows more complex and crowded, the need for large-scale control of environment and equipment will demand robotic hands at the helms of trains and boats and planes everywhere.

So much for the future being one in which there's no rush hour. Now it seems as if things are going to get so crowded only robots will be able to navigate their way through the gridlock.

Despite what many have thought though, the great robot workforce has failed to materialise meaning that for the time being at any rate, be the jobs menial or otherwise, us humans are just going to have to carry on workkkkk ...... iiinnn .... ggggg .... x'sfggsgdagbabcccd .. dd .... malfunction ... malfunction ...... must .... get ...... oil must .... get ..... oil.

5. My brain hurts

The notion of using one's brain while involved in 'work' is clearly a relatively new one if this prediction by Kate Field is anything to go by. It appeared in an 1893 article entitled 'Predictions For 1993', with the sub-heading, 'Four Bright Journalists Forecast The Future'.

> There has been a steady improvement in the condition of what is falsely called 'the labouring class', as though no one worked except the manual labourer. I only hope that the brain worker will be as well paid in 1993 as will be the manual labourer. ...

Doubtless she doesn't mean brain surgeons specifically, though they would come under the heading of brain worker, along with, one imagines, the likes of accountants, lawyers, stockbrokers and so on, all of whom have just about managed to claw their way up to the earning levels of manual labourers.

While Kate was clearly keen on brain work herself, a few years later, it was a matter of some concern to one Hans Friedenthal, especially when it was the likes of Kate who were doing it. Hans was a physiologist/anthropologist at the University of Berlin and, in 1914 he was somewhat troubled by the emancipation of women and especially what might happen if the ladies starting eschewing housework for work of a more cerebrally demanding nature. Here's what he was quoted as saying in a Berlin newspaper.

> Brain work will cause the 'new woman' to become bald while increasing masculinity and contempt for beauty will induce the growth of hair on the face. In the future therefore, women will be bald and wear long moustaches and patriarchal beards.

Hans clearly mixed up female intellectuals with female Eastern European shot putters, so he wasn't all wrong.

It's a simply astounding prediction; even more so when you discover that Hans wasn't immediately fired afterwards, rather he went on to become a professor, founded the 'Institute of Mankind Studies' and, wait for it, ran a marriage guidance council. Was there ever a man less qualified for that job?

Thinking about it though, one can only presume that having made his prediction, Hans believed the inverse also to be true, such that if men were to give up work and take on a more traditional female role, they would grow more hair on their head, less on their face, start developing breasts and lose their penises. Before you knew where you were, they'd be having babies and staying at home to look after them, so everything would be back to normal. No problem then, eh Hans?

6. Employmental

Having given the award of most optimistic person ever to would-be restaurateur H. Russell Brand, it would be unfair to take it away, but coming a close second are America's National Education Association who made a series of predictions in 1931 that were published *in The Literary Digest* under the heading 'What Shall We Be Like In 1950?'

Remember, 1931 was not a good time in America; it was a great time, though only in the great depression sense, so anything that could be said to cheer up the miserable hordes was more than welcome.

The predictions were said to be 'definite prophecies' – always an error – and with unemployment running at 15.9 per cent and rising, when it came to jobs the short term outlook could not have been bleaker. Long term though, according to the NEA, they could not have been better as they proudly trumpeted,

By 1950, there will be work for all.

As the unemployment rate rose the following year to 23.6 per cent and then 24.9 per cent the year after, no doubt there were many who rejoiced in thinking, 'great, only another 19 years to get through and I'll be able to put food on the table again'.

TRAVEL AND TRANSPORT

The moment we can sit up, we want to crawl. The moment we can crawl, we want to walk. The moment we can walk, we want to run. The moment we can run, we want to run faster, and the moment we can run faster, we want to strap on an anti-gravity thermo-nuclear powered jet pack and head off to Jupiter in less time than it currently takes to fly to Paris.

As a species we're obsessed with getting from A to B (often via C because of road works) as quickly as possible, in great comfort and with the minimum of fuss, effort and inconvenience. As the advert says, 'getting there is half the fun', though that does pre-suppose that getting back is the other half of the fun, in which case wherever you're actually going must be pretty miserable.

Nonetheless, we still want to get there and advances in technology have meant that on a good day, with a decent wind, no strikes, mechanical malfunctions, terrorist threats, weather problems, unforeseen circumstances or human errors we can now zip about the planet with a fair degree of speed and pleasure. And that's surely a good thing. In days of yore, some folk spent so much time commuting they didn't actually get to do any work because by the time they arrived at their workplace it was time to head home. This was beautiful for the workshy but less so for any industry or business.

There are those from the past who, should they be teleported through time to arrive in the 21st century – as some of them probably predicted would be possible by now – might just be a shade disappointed. 'Where are all the hovercars?' they might shout. Or, 'What do you mean I can't park my personal helicopter here?' Or even, 'Three hours to Manchester?! It was quicker in my day and I was travelling by stagecoach.'

It seems that just as we are in a hurry to get everywhere, they were in a hurry to predict just how much of a hurry we'd be in and hurriedly came up with transportation methods that have less chance of happening any time soon than Richard Branson has of traversing the globe in a balloon.

In short, yet more hot air.

1. Moving sidewalks, electric roller skates and footmobiles (basically, anything but walking)

As the old adage goes; why walk when you can hop onto a moving sidewalk? For many years, a city with non-static pavements was seen as the 'must have' item for any vision of the urban future, or urbuture as it's never been known. It's enough to make healthcare and exercise professionals choke on their tofu burgers as they rally to save walking from extinction. In their nightmares they envision all the calories piled on at breakfast, *staying on*, as, instead of ambulating to the station to go to work, we are propelled there via these mobile monstrosities. And their fears might well have been realised if planners working on the development of New York City in 1871 had had their way.

They were concerned about the city's congestion problems, which were pretty bad in those days – you could barely move for horse poo. Consequently, they proposed a network of moving underground sidewalks to carry New York's inhabitants around the city. They drew up plans for the system and presented them to the city's mayor, Seth Low, who was a reasonable man. He listened intently, scrupulously went through every detail of their proposal, offered them coffee and patisseries and then asked them to leave.

It was a blow, but not the knockout one that annoyingly fit and healthy people must have wished for because, even though the idea slunk away for a while, 29 years later it crept back. With the advent of the 20th century, the next generation of planners clearly felt they had a wave of ridiculous optimism on their side and proposed the moving walkways again, though this time for the sole use of travelling backwards and forwards under the Brooklyn Bridge. Once again their suggestion was rebuffed possibly in the following way – 'Why do we need a moving walkway under the Brooklyn Bridge in order to travel backwards and forwards from one side to the other when we can do exactly that, by walking *across* the selfsame Brooklyn Bridge?'

It was another blow, but, though reeling, the planners returned yet again in 1910 having revised their plans. (In reality, however, it is suspected that all they actually did was change the font and put them in a new folder.) Needless to say their vision of a walking-free New York was kicked into touch once again, and this time, for good.

Having had their three strikes and been given well and truly out, you'd have thought the experience of New York's planners would not have gone unheeded by their colleagues elsewhere in the land of the free but, if you did think that, you'd be wrong.

Over in Atlanta, Georgia, they'd followed events in New York very closely, and learnt precisely nothing from them, which is why in the 1920s The Beeler Organisation (a firm of engineers and consultants) drew up plans for a 'Continuous

Transit System', to be built beneath the city. The moving walk-ways of this system were to be divided into four lanes, the first of which did not in fact move, a cunning non-moving walkway, or simply, walkway.

This was a stationary point-of-embarkation lane for the ped-estrian who would then step on to the second lane, which was moving, at a whopping two miles an hour, slower than most people actually walk. So, if you fancied getting to work late you could stay on lane two, but the more adventurous might well have been enticed to skip over to lane three, which was really speeding along at a mighty four miles an hour, barely visible to the naked eye. Travelling on that lane would have been virtually extreme-non-walking, a whole new sport.

Incredibly though, for those lunatics who weren't speed-sated enough by lane three, a fourth lane was proposed which would go at, wait for it, a staggering 6 mph. It really was insanity squared, not least because the fourth lane also came equipped with seats, so that you could actually sit down while not walking. A moving sitway if you will.

The Beeler folk really had put a lot of work and effort into their vision of Atlanta's future, all of which went to waste when the project failed to be green lit. Indeed, it was red lit, and at the first set of lights, because the decision makers of the Atlanta municipality had seen the future of travel and it wasn't an underground platform. It was noisy, polluting and had four wheels.

Ultimately, it's probably quite a good thing that moving walkways never saw the light of day in America; if they had, the chances are that a large proportion of the population today would be morbidly obese.

So, the Twenties weren't going to be roaring to the sound of moving walkways, underground or otherwise, but that certainly didn't stop people foreseeing their creation in the future. Hugo Gernsback was predominantly a science fiction writer, but occa-sionally he'd venture into the realms of reality and attempt to make genuine predictions about the future. Ironically, a lot of these turned out to be science fiction, in particular those to be found in an article he wrote entitled, '50 Years From Now'. The 'Now' in question was 1925, so a simple calculation lets us know that he was predicting life in 1975, or 1987 if you can't add up. Hugo also envisaged a sizeable walking backlash and reckoned we'd all be not-walking on continuously moving platforms, but his vision made The Beeler Organisation's proposal seem positively tortoise-like.

> There will be three such moving platforms alongside of each other. The first platform will move only a few miles per hour, the second at eight or ten miles per hour, and the third at twelve or fifteen miles per hour. You step upon the slowest moving one from terra firma and move to the faster ones and take your seat.

Clearly all Hugo had done was take the Beeler Organisation's idea and add a few miles per hour to each lane, a cut and dried case of prediction plagiarism it would seem, though for some reason charges were never brought.

Gernsback obviously wasn't that bothered by health and safety issues either as attempting to disembark from a platform moving at 15 mph could result in some nasty accidents and most probably a death or two. You might get there more quickly, but not, perhaps, in one piece.

But Hugo had plenty more to offer when it came to transportation.

> Each pedestrian will roll on electric skates. ... An insulated wire running from the skate to the head or shoulder of the skater will be sufficient to take the power from the radio power line, and we shall then all be propelled electrically at a pace at least four or five times as fast as we walk today.

Essentially what he appears to have predicted here are

individual roller skate trams. Curious enough in themselves, but it seems odd that having already predicted one thing that would allow people to travel four or five times as fast as they could walk, he then went on to predict something else that would allow them to do exactly the same, only with a greater chance of electrocution.

It was a ridiculous prediction anyway; if he'd had any genuine insight into the Seventies he would have predicted electric skates with platform soles.

Individualised contraptions to eradicate the horror of walking were nothing new though. Back in 1900 a newspaper in the American state of Indiana ran the following headline:

No one will walk – all will have wheels.

They were not predicting that one day we would all evolve to have wheels on the end of our legs, rather that we would all be charging around on natty-looking footmobiles.

The Footmobile – the must-have accessory for the
20th century that no one had.

If only the creator of the Segway had been privy to this prediction, he could have saved himself all that time, effort, money, ridicule, and ultimately, death.

Footmobiles look as if they were thought up by a child, and a very young one at that. However, incredibly the Electric Monroe Company did start to manufacture them and, though sales figures don't exist, it's probably safe to say they weren't exactly rushed off their feet.

2. A life on the ocean wave (that never happened)

A recurring theme linking many predictions is that of futuristic technology becoming available to 'the masses'. It was generally assumed that the huge advances yet to be made would benefit everyone, whereas in fact the reality, of course, is that they only benefit those who can afford them.

One such prediction was boldly made in a 1958 article that appeared in the *Chicago Tribune*. The paper stated that,

> The luxury of yachting may be within the reach of almost everyone in the world of tomorrow.

On what basis did they make their prediction about mass yacht-owning? Did they think the price of metal and wood would fall to zero in the future, or that local shipbuilders would stop charging for their services? Or perhaps that we would all be overwhelmed by a huge desire to dress up in vintage naval uniforms and take to the high seas? No, instead they claim that:

> Mass production of low-cost plastic hulls will be made possible by the use of guns that spray the plastic.

That's cleared that one up then; instead of spending Sundays washing cars, tomorrow's children could earn some extra pocket money by using plastic-spraying guns to make boat hulls. In fact, if the guns themselves were plastic they could use them to make more guns.

The article goes on to explain the ingenious way in which this sprayed yacht will be powered:

> The family car will be used for motive power. When the yachtsman of the future drives his auto into the cradle of his new marine creation the engine will be in place. The rear wheels will rest on a roller linked to the propeller. The driver will put the car in gear, step on the accelerator, and presto – he'll be yachting.

Yes, unwittingly they appear to have predicted *Chitty Chitty Bang Bang*, with possibly a nod even to Dick Van Dyke's rather plastic performance.

It's a lovely thought, though one wonders just how congested things might get as we all hop aboard our yachts, waving contentedly at the five million other yachts in the canal leading towards the shops in the city centre.

Of course, half a century earlier things were somewhat different. Back then only the very few had their own yachts and if you wanted a leisurely nautical experience you'd have to spend it in the company of many others aboard a massive ocean-going liner such as RMS *Adriatic* perhaps. At the helm of this impressive sea beast was one Captain E.J. Smith who, in 1907, asserted that shipbuilding was such a perfect art that absolute disaster, involving the passengers on a great modern liner, was quite unthinkable. Whatever happened, he contended, there would be time before the vessel sank to save the lives of every person on board.

> I will go a bit further. I will say that I cannot imagine any condition which could cause a ship to founder. ... Modern shipbuilding has gone beyond that.

Smith did go a bit further. Five years later he arrived at a new and exciting job; captain of the *Titanic*. Yes, that *Titanic*.

His prediction does suggest an alternative explanation as to what might have happened though. Perhaps Captain Smith hadn't in fact intended to go down with his ship. Perhaps he was halfway through slipping on his wife's favourite dress in the hope of hopping on board a lifeboat in accordance with the 'women and children first rule', when he suddenly remembered his not-so-prophetic words and chose death instead.

To add insult to fatal injury, after the *Titanic* sank, some of its surviving passengers returned to England, on board Captain Smith's old charge, the *Adriatic*.

The only solace for Captain Smith was that he wasn't alone in his views. As Mrs Sylvia Caldwell boarded the ship she was confidently told by a crew member.

God himself could not sink this ship!

On the morning of 15 April 1912, with the *Titanic* somewhere out at sea in its death throes, Philip Franklin, Vice-President of White Star Line, the company that owned the ship, said,

The boat is unsinkable.

As they say, pride comes before a crash into an iceberg.

The master of prediction and sci-fi writing genius, H.G. Wells also dipped his toe into the waters of wrongness in 1901 when, on hearing of plans to make a submergible craft, he exclaimed,

My imagination refuses to see any sort of submarine doing anything but suffocate its crew and floundering at sea.

Right, so he could imagine a time machine, a Martian invasion and an invisible man, but not a submarine. Perhaps they should have sought the opinion of Jules Verne instead.

Some forward-thinkers get a general concept right, but fall

short on the details. An example of this was postulated by the fantastically creative and brainy team behind a publication called *The Electrical Experimenter*. Its July 1917 edition had this headline on the cover: 'OLD U.S. BATTLESHIPS TO THE FRONT.' The picture accompanying it was of an old US Warship that had been souped-up with four huge metallic wheels, its hull covered in tough metal. The idea it seems is that by fixing the wheels on to the craft it would be able to come out of the water on to dry land, whereupon it would prove a useful addition to the US army.

As an early attempt at recycling it was admirable, but as an early attempt at helping end World War One, it was unusable, which is quite possibly why it never happened.

3. Trains, trains and train-mobiles

Sticking to what you know and trust is one of mankind's oldest foibles and can often stand in the way of technological advancement. Rather than embrace the new, there are many who rush to predict its uselessness, demise and folly. When it came to trains there were so many who decried these monsters that the world's largest humble pie needed to be baked and eaten, without relish of course.

First out of the depot was English periodical *The Quarterly Review* which, in 1825, declared:

> What can be more palpably absurd than the prospect held out of locomotives travelling twice as fast as stagecoaches?

Locomotives travelling three times as fast as stagecoaches (or toads pulling a stagecoach while singing 'Rule Britannia')? Mind you, you can see where these naysayers were coming from. Horses were such an established method of transport and locomotive travel such a complex idea that for many the idea of a carriage rolling along on tracks at high speed was a completely foreign and, in some cases, terrifyingly unrealistic idea. Accepting trains were inevitable was a bit like us saying today that in a hundred years electrified mini-skateboards will be able to cross the Atlantic Ocean in three minutes. Satirical writers of the future would have a field day with our perceived stupidity as they traversed the globe on their mini skateboards.

Also that year the building of a railway between Liverpool and Manchester was proposed which caused outrage, as reported by Samuel Smiles in his biography of George 'The Rocket' Stephenson.

> ... pamphlets were written and newspapers were hired to revile the railway. It was declared that its formation would prevent cows grazing and hens laying. The poisoned air from the locomotives would kill birds as they flew over them, and render the preservation of pheasants and foxes no longer possible. Householders adjoining the projected line were told that their houses would be burnt up by the fire thrown from the engine-chimneys, while the air around would be polluted by clouds of smoke. There would no longer be any use for horses; and if railways extended, the species would become extinguished, and oats and hay unsalable commodities. Travelling by road would be rendered highly dangerous, and country inns would be ruined. Boilers would burst and blow passengers to atoms. But there was always this consolation to wind up with – that the weight of the locomotive would completely prevent its moving, and that railways, even if made, could never be worked by steam-power!

Hard to know where to start really. It's possible that this is the most incorrect prediction ever made, being, as it is, wrong on no fewer than 15 counts. No doubt many of the pamphlets were written by future politicians. One prediction that stands out though is that after bursting, the boilers would *'blow passengers to atoms'*. Well quite, coal is a very volatile and unstable substance, the slightest jolt causes it to explode doesn't it?

It's also worth drawing attention to the prediction that there would no longer be any uses for horses. It's ridiculous of course, there are plenty of other uses for horses, meat and glue to name but two.

Across the water and New York Governor Martin Van Buren was also freaking out about train travel, so much so that in 1829 he fired off a hysterical letter, in both senses of the word, to President Andrew Jackson, making three apocalyptical predictions.

> One. If canal boats are supplanted by 'railroads,' serious unemployment will result. Captains, cooks, drivers, hostlers, repairmen, and lock tenders will be left without means of livelihood, not to mention the numerous farmers now employed in growing hay for horses.

Herein we see the inspiration for the John Le Carré novel, *Tinker, Tailor, Soldier, Spy* which, in its original incarnation is widely believed to have been Captain, Cook, Driver, Hostler. Frankly, it's unlikely that President Jackson read further than this paragraph as the letter no doubt led to him feeling particularly hostled.

> Two. Boat builders would suffer and towline, whip and harness makers would be left destitute.

Yet more unemployment and misery predicted, though, of course, boat builders continue to find gainful employ building, among other things, super-yachts for billionaires, while whip and harness makers still eke out a decent living supplying goods to the S&M trade. Sadly, towline makers haven't really had a great time of it latterly, though some do reasonably well in the tug-of-war market.

> Three. Canal boats are absolutely essential to the defense of the United States. In the event of the expected trouble with England,

the Erie Canal would be the only means by which we could ever move the supplies so vital to waging modern war.

The expected trouble with England? Okay, so perhaps Britain and America didn't quite have a 'special relationship' yet, but by 1829 peace had broken out between the two sides. Van Buren's prediction of hostilities may well have been based on false information and there's no way the two countries would wage war with themselves or anyone else based on information which turns out to have been incorrect is there?

Another choo-choo scaremonger was a certain Dionysius Lardner, a science writer and teacher, who asserted that:

Rail travel at high speed is not possible, because passengers would die of asphyxia.

Hardly surprising then that most of his pupils failed their Trains GCSE.

Dionysius' prediction is one of a number made about the harmful effect of rail travel on people's health. It's a view shared by Bavaria's Royal College of Doctors which claimed that the rapid movement of trains would cause 'brain trouble' among travellers, and 'vertigo' among those who looked at moving trains. So not only would passengers suffer greatly, but train-spotters as well – not all bad news then.

Another who foresaw a health problem of sorts was French Physicist and Astronomer Dominique François Arago who claimed that,

... transport by railroad car would result in the emasculation of our troops and would deprive them of the option of the great marches which have played such an important role in the triumph of our armies.

Presumably then he'd rather the troops arrived exhausted,

covered in blisters and late for battle, rather than have their masculinity challenged. That's the French for you.

The good, or not so good, Bavarian doctors' opinion, probably had some influence over King William I of Prussia who confidently decreed that,

> No one will pay good money to get from Berlin to Potsdam in one hour when he can ride his horse there in one day for free.

Yes indeed, why would anyone want to travel the 15 miles from Potsdam to Berlin in an hour? Where's yer Prussia now, eh King Willie?

So, predictions about the dangers of rail travel were fervent, terrifying and ultimately completely useless and thus, once rail travel took off, were replaced by predictions that were nonsensical, insane and completely useless, such as the one encapsulated in a British Pathe Newsreel of 1932.

This delightful film is entitled, *Flying Trains* and therein lies quite a considerable clue as to the nature of the prediction. It's a silent movie and begins with the following words onscreen.

> With the successful trials of the rapid 'Zepp Train,' Germany is experimenting further with various units to ascertain the most efficient shape for high speed transport.

All very exciting and no doubt expectations among the watching audiences were high as they imagined images of a wildly futuristic space-age device, whereas in fact what they're shown is a model train with a propeller attached to the front and a rudder to the back on an old-fashioned model railway set. We're then told,

> Bodies and tracks may vary, but they all rely on propellers for tractive effort and speeds of 150 miles an hour are prophesied.

Perhaps, but not on a model railway set. It gets better though, as next we're treated to a man putting another model train on to the tracks, this time with aeroplane wings attached to it. This then appears to take part in some sort of race with the propeller train and a non-bastardised train, which, surprise, surprise, it wins.

Unsurprisingly however, in spite of the reel's breathless excitement and novelty value, the train with wings never got past the experimental stage or, indeed the 'Dad's got a model railway in the attic and is doing something odd with it' stage.

The need to reach ever-increasing speeds is a common theme in transportation; after all, what's the point in getting somewhere at a relaxed, leisurely pace when you can get there at breakneck speed and almost break your neck in doing so?

Hence in 1956 a certain Mr Oscar G. Burch, Vice-President in charge of research for the Owens-Illinois Glass Company, predicted that trains of the future would, as reported in *Modern Mechanix* magazine,

> whip passengers vast distances ... at speeds and in comfort far surpassing that of modern air travel.

Mr Burch was referred to as a '... *very sound and serious-minded engineer*', which meant he could postulate any outlandish theories and be listened to. He foresaw a future in which trains travelled inside tubes made of, wait for it, glass. Yes, that's right, the very same glass that the company he worked for just happened to manufacture. So, with no self-interest whatsoever, Burch predicted that trains would zip through a 'Glass Sheath', at speeds of 300 mph powered by compressed air that would shoot them from coast to coast, combining the speed of flight with the comfort of ground travel. It's brilliant, not least because putting trains inside glass tubes would finally rid the world of the terrible affliction that is 'leaves on the line'.

Sadly, it is yet to happen, as are any of the other predictions made by Burch and his company, all of which have one thing in common. See if you can spot what it is.

> They see the day fast approaching when the pressure of increasing world population will lead to the erection of entire glass cities in desert and arctic regions – cities constructed on glass columns, enclosed in glass domes, heated and air conditioned by atomic power. Inside the glass cities of the future will be glass homes, glass furniture and glass cars, planes and trains – all combining the structural strength of steel with the transparency and beauty of crystal.

Less a prediction really and more of an advert.

4. Up, up and away with the fairies

In 1784, not long after the Montgolfier brothers had launched the first hot air balloon, the public were so alarmed by the phenomenon that the French government had to issue a proclamation to allay people's fears about the craft. It was new; it rose into the air; it was big and frightening – just like the future.

In 1847, in his book *Les Cents Merveilles des Sciences des Arts* (Look it up. Oh alright then, *The Hundred Wonders of Science and Art*) French writer M. De Marles, stated that:

> It has been demonstrated by the fruitlessness of a thousand attempts that it is not possible for a machine, moving under its own power, to generate enough force to raise itself, or sustain itself in the air.

Aaargh, if only he'd waited for the thousandth and first attempt! Derision at attempts to defy gravity were not to be quelled though; indeed they had only just begun. Over in America folk were equally adamant that we were destined to keep our feet firmly on the ground.

Put these three indisputable facts together:

One: There is a low limit of weight, certainly not much beyond fifty pounds, beyond which it is impossible for an animal to fly. Nature has reached this limit, and with her utmost effort has failed to pass it.

Two: The animal machine is far more effective than any we can hope to make; therefore the limit of the weight of a successful flying machine cannot be more than fifty pounds.

Three: The weight of any machine constructed for flying, including fuel and engineer, cannot be less than three or four hundred pounds. Is it not demonstrated that a true flying machine, self-raising, self-sustaining, self-propelling, is physically impossible?

This beautiful example of illogical logic, or as philosophers call it, bollocks, was the work of Joseph LeConte (steady), who at the time, 1888, was Professor of Natural History at the University of California.

It might be thought that such a statement would result in Joseph's immediate sacking and subsequent shunning by the scientific community, but nothing could be further from the truth. In 1892 he was made president of the American Association for the Advancement of Science and after his death in 1901 the LeConte Memorial Lodge was named in his honour. Oh, and LeConte Glacier, LeConte Canyon, LeConte Divide, LeConte Falls and Mount LeConte are all named after him as well. As are LeConte Middle School in Hollywood, LeConte Hall on the UC Berkeley campus, LeConte Avenue in Berkeley, and LeConte Avenue which runs along the south of UCLA. It's only surprising that there isn't a company called LeConte Tours offering trips to see all the LeConte memorials, by plane of course.

In Britain, Lord Kelvin, that giant of science and president of the esteemed British Royal Society, threw his hat into the ring in 1895, by declaring that,

Heavier than air flying machines are not possible.

Okay, so he's made his position quite clear; the last thing to do would be to invite him to join the Aeronautical Society. But that's exactly what happened the following year, though they probably wish they hadn't bothered as he refused, saying,

I have not the smallest molecule of faith in aerial navigation other than ballooning or of expectation of good results from any of the trials we hear of.

Lord Kelvin's loss as, by all accounts, they did lovely teacakes at Aeronautical Society meetings.

He hadn't finished though. In case anyone still wasn't sure as to where he stood on air travel, in a newspaper interview in 1902 his Lordship predicted that,

No balloon and no aeroplane will ever be practically successful.

And this just a year before the first, very practically successful flight, not to mention, a year later, the even more practically successful use of balloons at children's birthday parties.

However, even those at the forefront of flight creation had their doubts. Wilbur Wright – who with his brother Orville was responsible for that first practically successful flight in 1903 – remarked just two years before this success that:

Man will not fly for 50 years.

As well as the obvious irony in that comment, there's also

a less obvious irony in the fact that even after the Wright brothers' first flight there were many who didn't believe it had actually happened; in particular over in France where Ernest Archdeacon, founder of the Aero-Club de France (you should be able to translate that one yourselves), didn't believe a word of it and went on to predict that,

... the French would make the first public demonstration of powered flight.

What he should have said though was that the French would make one of the first public demonstrations of being very embarrassed about powered flight, something he may have considered saying in 1908 when the Wright brothers popped over to France to demonstrate their flying machines.

Naturally, despite the actual reality of flight, there were still many who said it would never happen, such as Sir Stanley Mosley who stated categorically in 1905 that, '*it is complete nonsense to believe flying machines will ever work*', the engineering editor of *The Times* who said in 1906, '*All attempts at artificial aviation are not only dangerous to human life, but foredoomed to failure from the engineering standpoint*', and Lord Haldane, Britain's minister of war who went with, '*the aeroplane will never fly*', in 1907.

In 1917, 16 years after Wilbur Wright's unfortunate prediction, and 14 years after that first flight, his brother Orville decided it was time he got in on the act by proudly declaring that:

The aeroplane will help peace in more ways than one ... it will have a tendency to make war impossible!

Clearly Orville didn't possess an accurate crystal ball, because if he'd had one, a vicious Luftwaffe plane would have soared out from its cloudy depths and blown him to pieces.

It would be very wrong though to confine our investigations to those of the solely verbal or written kind because many a barking mad prediction was made by those of a more visual bent.

In Germany at the beginning of the 20th century a series of postcards were produced that depicted what the artist thought life would be like in the year 2000, and when it came to air travel, personalised flying machines and personalised airships were very much the order of the day.

Not to be outdone by the Germans (well, not for a few years at any rate), in 1910 the French artist Villemard brought out his own set of predictive postcards looking ahead to the year 2000 which included some real gems of the genre. In particular he foresaw flying police and flying firemen. Obviously he didn't predict flying ambulance crews, because they'd have to stay on the ground attending to all the injured police and firemen who'd fallen out of the sky. Interesting also to note that neither prediction led to fears of huge unemployment among ladder makers.

His best, depending on how you look at it, prediction though was something like this . . .

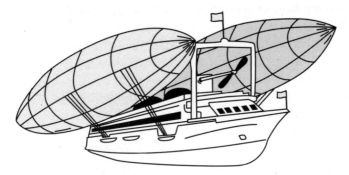

. . . the double airship ship. It has many benefits such as allowing you to choose whether you want to get seasick or airsick and helping those unsure if they want to join the Navy or the RAF to make up their mind. Is it a ship? Is it a plane? No, it's a bleeding postcard.

Once air travel did take off (apologies), as with trains, the predictions became less about its impossibilities and more about its limitless possibilities such as the article that appeared in the *Nevada State Journal* in 1919 under the headline, 'Giant Air Cruisers To Link Cities Of The World, Predicts British Expert'.

With no little excitement, the journal reports Sir Trevor Dawson, managing director of airship manufacturers Vickers Ltd, claim that every city in the world will soon be reachable from London within only ten days. The paper then prints an 'Aerial Time Table' the highlights of which are as follows.

London to New York – 2 to 2 and a half days
London to Cape Town – 5 and a half days
London to Perth, Australia – 7 days.

Not so much travelling at the speed of sound as travelling at the speed of a cow being pushed in a wheelbarrow.

As things progressed though, and the travelling time between cities became a little quicker, many began to wonder just how fast it was possible to go. In the years following World War Two, aviation designers and scientists found themselves asking the same question, perhaps slightly guiltily: surely the technology behind the atom bomb can be used for a slightly less destructive purpose? And so was born the idea of the Atomic Airplane. In addition to storing a varied food and drinks trolley, this vessel would also contain its very own nuclear reactor; Chernobyl with wings.

By 1956, five companies were exploring this avenue and a 1958 edition of *National Geographic* magazine foresaw these companies,

> ... testing the reactions of crewmen during long confinement in a simulated nuclear aircraft cockpit.

The fact that they may emerge as incandescent skeletons with partial coverings of skin didn't seem to enter into the equation, though to be fair, some of the companies were aware of the inherent danger of working on such a craft and suggested storing the reactor in the back of the plane while placing the crew in a very long nose at the front.

Great advice, somewhat like telling someone to stand a couple of streets away from the epicentre of a nuclear bomb blast. But still, companies insisted it was possible to create these planes. One company came up with the Silver Arrow Atomic Airplane that they said would travel at 10,000 miles per hour. Because of different time zones, this plane would leave New York at midday and arrive in LA at 9 a.m. – giving the passenger a travelling time of, according to the company, *'minus 3 hours!'* Perhaps, but they forgot to add, 'and a life expectancy of three minutes'.

The matter won't go away though, and as recently as 2008, Ian Poll, a British professor of aerospace engineering said,

> I think nuclear-powered aeroplanes are the answer beyond 2050
> … but I accept it would take about 30 years to persuade the
> public of the need to fly on them.

That's quite an advertising campaign then: 'Fly Nuclear and arrive with that all-over warm glow'.

For planes then it was all about speed, whereas when it came to their chums in the helicopter world the focus was more on personalisation; though no one suggested anything quite along the lines of those postcards, sanity wasn't entirely the order of the day.

Under the headline, 'The Future of the Helicopter', a 1955 edition of Japan's *Pacific Stars and Stripes* magazine, made a couple of predictions that didn't exactly fly. First up was the portable helicopter or 'Hoppi-copter'.

> Another unusual whirlybird is the 'portable helicopter,' a four-
> bladed rotor and engine weighing 60 pounds. To fly, the operator
> simply straps the contraption on his back, starts the motor and
> takes off.

An interesting definition of portable here.

A minor issue though, because if successful, well, the practical uses are manifold surely.

> In war the infantryman might use it for airborne assaults. In
> peacetime the Dodger fan could take in a double header without
> having to fight stadium crowds on the way to the game.

Brilliant, it can be used for killing people or for going to baseball games. In fact, to ensure you get a seat for a really big game where tickets are scarce, it could probably be used for both at the same time.

Also predicted was a 'flying platform', a sort of inverse helicopter with rotating fans underneath a base.

Inexpensive and so simple to operate it could serve as an assault boat for the individual soldier, it also may be the businessman's speedy coupe of the future.

Readiness for World War Three was clearly a pre-occupation back then, though there does seem to be some confusion over the definition of the word 'boat', and quite possibly 'coupe'.

'But where are the ladies in all this?' you cry. Well, for them we unveil the Shopper Hopper as premiered in 1959 in the *Chicago Tribune*'s regular 'Closer Than We Think!' comic strip.

A kind of 'flying carpet' may be the answer to the problem of personal transportation in the future. The flying platforms would be suitable for such uses as low altitude hops to neighboring shops.

What we have here is a classic example of a prediction in which technology moves forward, but male/female stereotypes remain firmly stuck in the 1950s.

Clearly, the editors of the paper decided that your basic personal flying machine would be flown by men as they go to work or go about their manly business of travelling to poker games and cinemas to watch films with medium levels of aggression, while the women of the future, still needing to provide a hearty meal for their husbands when they return home, would jet about in a shopper hopper.

It was designed with the fairer sex in mind. The overarching principle is simplicity, thus allowing the ladyfolk to gossip away to their hearts' content and, in terms of controls, there was just the one lever. Probably a little complex for gals, but until the Shopper Hopper Mark II with male robot driver is developed, they'll just have to try and make sure they don't get into too much of a tizz flying it. No doubt, though, there will still be the occasional accident, leaving men to decry, 'bloody women fliers!'

Interestingly, the lever is slightly phallic, thereby sending an unconscious signal to the woman that it's been a while since she touched her husband's penis and she should probably let him have his evil way with her soon.

In terms of these vehicles actually becoming a reality, the article continues with:

> Military models of these 'hoppers' have already been developed at Piasecki Aircraft and Chrysler. The flat platforms are lifted by air blasts through ducts at the bottom. The vanes of the ducts are movable, to permit control of direction. These vehicles would hover like helicopters and move at city traffic speeds. Construction would be simple, and costs could be kept low enough for civilian requirements.

Well, despite what the paper says about the military having already invented hoppers, there is no record of US personnel in 'Nam jumping into one, nipping off to the local Saigon Sainsbury's for a takeout lunch and returning in time to napalm a nearby village.

And so, via the moving walkway, footmobile, winged train, flying police officer and shopper hopper, we arrive at the jet-pack. Or rocket belt. Or rocket pack. Or jet flying belt. Whatever you choose to call it, it's the most prized totem of the futuristic predictor and scientist, a symbol of a new dawn of civilisation when we'll all be able to fly. It's a wondrous dream indeed, with one small problem; it's not actually a dream. Jetpacks have existed and still do in various guises.

Such a thing was first imagined in the late 1920s in *The Amazing Stories* science fiction magazine and then popped up, or jetted up, in various films subsequently until, as they were staring defeat in the face at the end of World War Two, the Nazis made the first real attempt to get one off the ground. They drew up plans for the Himmelstürmer, or Skystormer, and were just about to try it out when the idiots foolishly went and lost the war.

The prototype and plans were not lost however, and ended up in the hands of the American company Bell Aerosystems, who in the early Sixties made the first working jetpack.

The point about jetpack predictions therefore is not so much about the things themselves as the promise of the revolution they will bring about to our lives.

> I believe in our lifetime we will see jetpacks used in commuter service between office and home, in the police department and individual family life.

Thus predicted Robert May, Bell Aerosystem's Jetpack project manager in the Sixties. No doubt then he was somewhat disappointed in 1970 when Bell sold all of their Jetpack patents for a knockdown price to another company.

And that, in a nutshell, is the history of the jetpack. To date no one has managed to overcome the problems of air traffic control, weather, pollution and of course, fly-by muggings, so despite the fact that many have since been developed and, if you have a spare $100,000 you can currently buy one (check out www.martinjetpack.com for one), birds, bees and flying fish can rest easy and relax, secure in the knowledge that, for the time being at least, we won't be further polluting their environment with ourselves. Once again predictors got the concept right but in terms of development and scope were way off the pace.

5. Auto-idiocy

The minute someone makes a prediction about a future technology, someone hails it as the world's greatest invention while someone else decries it as dangerous, untrustworthy or evil. And so it was when the idea of the car started being bandied about with increasing regularity.

One of the first to dampen any excitement there might have

been about the development of cars, was American magazine *The Literary Digest* which felt it their duty, in 1899, to make clear that,

> The ordinary 'horseless carriage' is at present a luxury for the wealthy; and although its price will probably fall in the future, it will never, of course, come into as common use as the bicycle.

It's a delightful use of the ever so slightly overly pompous, 'of course', that casual certainty which makes it all the more delicious to note how very, very wrong they, of course, were. Four years later and this prediction was made.

> The horse is here to stay but the automobile is only a novelty – a fad.

This is a particular gem because it was made by the president of the Michigan Savings Bank on being asked for his advice by one Horace Rackham.

Now at the time Horace was a lawyer who had just taken on a new client, to wit a certain Henry Ford – yes, him from the Model T et al. – and the question he'd asked his bank manager was, 'Should I invest $5,000 in the Ford Motor Company?' The manager replied in the negative. Brilliantly, Horace didn't follow the bank manager's advice and scraped the 5k together to buy the shares, which he sold in 1919 for, wait for it, *twelve and a half million dollars*, probably the same amount as the bank manager's bonus that year.

If the bank manager felt like a complete twat, however – and he should have done – he could console himself with the fact that he wasn't alone.

A few years later in 1909, the readers of *Scientific American* magazine were subjected to the following woefully incorrect prediction:

That the automobile has practically reached the limit of its development is suggested by the fact that during the past year no improvements of a radical nature have been introduced.

In essence what they're saying is that we should all still be driving around in this little hot rod:

We now turn our headlights onto two predicted methods of transport that most certainly have come to pass; the flying car and the driverless car. Where the truth departs from several of these predictions lies in the realm of the popularity and widespread use of these travelling modes, not to mention the safety and possible instantaneous death aspects associated with their usage.

Eddie Rickenbacker was an American fighter pilot during World War One who went on to become an automotive designer and racing car driver, so it seems only right that he should make one of the first hopeless predictions about flying cars, which he duly did in 1924.

In the combined automobile airplane I see a machine that is not greatly different from the present day motor car. ... The wings will fold back along the sides of the car when driving along the

street and will have sufficient space to lift the car off the ground
at a moderate take off speed.

Fair point, it isn't greatly different to the motor car, apart from,
of course, the foldaway wings and the fact that it can fly.

It does beg the question though, how will cities adapt to
this new fangled machine? Thankfully, Eddie's way ahead of
us.

It would not take a great stretch of imagination to foresee muni-
cipalities regulating the height of buildings to uniformity, the
streets to be bridged, in order to form one vast landing field in
the center of each city for flying machines. The landing fields or
tops of the buildings could be connected with the street level by
elevators so that a machine alighting could descend to the street
and be driven about as an automobile. At the end of the business
day it would be driven back to the elevator and lifted to the roof
to take off for the homeward flight.

Essentially he reckons city centres will become runways with
huge lifts ferrying the carplanes to and from the take off and
landing points. Nothing nuts about that at all, as Eddie is quick
to point out.

Such a forecast is more than pure fancy. It is founded on present
progress in automobile and airplane design.

If Eddie had seen a production line of car/plane lifts he kept
quiet about it. Either way his vision of uniform building heights
and vast landing fields never got past check in.

In Britain, respected journalist and writer Philip Gibbs
managed to make himself slightly less respected by positing
the following in 1928:

In less than twenty-five years ... the motor-car will be obsolete, because the aeroplane will run along the ground as well as fly over it.

A little wide of the runway that one.

But a bad idea just won't go away it seems and after funding experiments into carplanes/planecars which resulted in a pilot being killed, no less an authority than Henry Ford still remained convinced that their introduction was a certainty.

Mark my word. A combination airplane and motor car is coming. You may smile. But it will come.

Not sure about smiling, laughing hysterically might be a better response.

By 1975 the carplane brigade was still going strong, and counted among its number Arthur C. Clarke who predicted that by the year 2000:

A road sign of the future is likely to read 'No wheeled vehicles on the highway.' Cars will float on air, bringing about the passing of the wheel.

It's an odd little curio this one because if there are flying cars, why would they not allow ordinary, wheeled cars to drive on the ground? It's not as if the two vehicles are battling for the same space is it?

As noted, the flying car is a reality and every few months some zany designer/engineer/publicity-hungry jaded executive, introduces the world to a new version. There are loads of companies developing them inspired no doubt by one of the first, the Model 118 Convair Car.

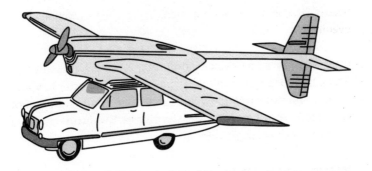

No one is quite sure what the predicted sales of this monstrosity were, but its first flight ended in a crash landing and though the second was marginally more successful, for some reason it's reported that, after it, enthusiasm for the project waned.

Driverless cars first made a significant dent into human consciousness at the 1939 New York World's Fair. Should you have wandered over to the Transportation Zone and stumbled upon the Futurama exhibit, you'd have found yourself strapped into a moving chair and hoisted into the air, so that you could look down upon a vast depiction of an area of the United States, in miniature. Essentially, a model village, in among which was a highway with electric cars moving along it powered by circuits embedded in the roadway and controlled by radio. Or Scalextric. So, what we have here is an incorrect prediction accidentally being correct about something that it didn't predict.

Moving on to the late Fifties and we find a straightforwardly incorrect prediction in an American advert for electricity put out by America's Independent Electric Light and Power Companies.

ELECTRICITY MAY BE THE DRIVER. One day your car may speed along an electric super-highway, its speed and steering automatically controlled by electronic devices embedded in the road. Highways will be made safe – by electricity! No traffic jam ... no collisions ... no driver fatigue.

No way.

Around the same time Disney decided to get in on the act with a programme called *Magic Highway USA*. One can only wonder at how they rejoiced when someone came up with that rhyme.

Part of the show was dedicated to the future of transportation and depicts your classic space age city of the future with, of course, driverless cars.

> As father chooses the route in advance on a push-button selector, electronics take over complete control. Progress can be accurately checked on a synchronized scanning map. With no driving responsibility, the family relaxes together. En route business conferences are conducted by television.

There's that fantastic Fifties sexism again, it's political correctness not gone mad. But they hadn't finished yet.

> On entering the city the family separates. Father to his office, Mother and son to the shopping center.

By, 'the family separates' they don't mean that Mum and Dad split up – divorce was practically illegal then – they mean that the driverless car splits in two and each half goes off in a different direction.

It's all quite appealing really, until there's a power cut and half of the city are wiped out in related road rage incidents.

The 1964 New York World's Fair sort of suggested driverless cars by ferrying people around in ... driverless cars, though it was more of a fairground ride than the real thing – not very different to what was on display in 1939 really. But in the late Seventies the first actual driverless car appeared in Japan followed shortly afterwards by the TV show *Knight Rider*, which featured a driverless car being controlled by a huge knob.

Driverless vehicles are a subject of multiple newspaper

features, each one extolling the increased accuracy and safety features of the latest prototype. And in some places they are already in use – for example a self-driving airport shuttle bus that takes passengers from the terminal building to the plane steps, using much of the sensory and electrical functions the forecasters suggested. Those heady predictors then succeeded where many failed; they predicted an invention that did see the light of day. Once again though, where they fell down was the extent to which their futuristic vehicles would be put to use.

In spite of a battery of tests and endless clean bills of safety being pronounced, driverless cars are not a standard feature on any of the world's main thoroughfares – yet. In part this is due to our increasing reliance on gadgets and gadgetry. That lovely thing called 'human error' is gradually being phased out of our lives to the point where we are required to make almost no decisions about our daily rituals and undertakings. It won't be long before we forget how to boil an egg or urinate for ourselves. And wherever we're reliant on technology there are lovely people in dimly-lit airless rooms who dedicate themselves to upending us.

Come on; if a GPS unit can be hacked into to direct an unsuspecting, non-map-using motorist to drive straight into a river, think of the fun that could be had with a fully automated car. If such vehicles were ever allowed on to the open road in great numbers, it surely wouldn't be long before some evil keyboard pounders were sending the vehicles up lamp posts or reversing down the wrong side of a dual carriageway. The passengers onboard one of these vehicles might well be able to sleep while their car whizzed them towards their destination, but they'd most certainly be dead on arrival.

EDUCATION

Apart from maybe Josef Fritzl, we all want the best for our children. We send them off to school in the hope that they learn, not only how to give Chinese burns and play kiss chase, but also to amass the great knowledge that our forebears have gathered through the ages. In so doing we are making a prediction of our own, one that looks to the future and sees that young, nervous child taking its first steps through the school gates, emerging many years later as an intelligent, well-adjusted human being, equipped and ready to conquer the world.

We're not going to be around much longer than three score and ten years (unless you believe some of the life span predictions from the Health and the Human Body chapter, see pp. 58–63, which you really shouldn't) so it will probably be up to that next generation to sort out the planet; to be honest, if they do the job a tenth of one per cent better than us, they'll be doing exceedingly well.

Education is seen by many as the greatest of all possible life chances; get a good education and you can do anything. Realistically that tends to be true only for people who are born into stability or affluence, but some of the most disadvantaged in society *do* manage to break free from their shackles and achieve great success thanks to an inspirational teacher or the ability to stay awake through thousands of hours of deathly boring algebra lessons. In short, humans predict that institutions such as schools, colleges and universities will be part of a process that creates a better future. Hmm, yes, well, just as more often than not that prediction falls some way wide of the mark; so it is with many of the predictions about the type of learning that goes on within these establishments.

Ironically, these predictions are often made by people who are well-educated themselves, yet despite their studies and numerous qualifications, time and time again these deluded souls add up two and two and make five; or in some cases nineteen and three quarters.

It's a disgrace and they should all be thoroughly ashamed of themselves. They've let their teachers down, they've let themselves down, but most of all they've let the whole world of predictions down. In fact they should all stay behind and see us later, even though many of them are now dead.

If those who can, do, and those who can't, teach, then those who make predictions about education, really shouldn't. In short, the message is clear and is one that teachers the world over have known for centuries; could do better.

1. Bottom of the class (F–)

Give me a child until he is seven and I will give you the man.

So says the famous maxim most often attributed to the Jesuit Francis Xavier, and as predictions go it's a little too general to be deemed entirely hopeless, but there are those who make a great case for its inclusion in this book by being given the child at an early age and giving back an entirely different and wildly inaccurate man.

One such person blessed with the power of very limited perception was Albert Einstein's teacher who, in 1895 said the following to Bertie's dad, Hermann Einstein.

It doesn't matter what he does, he will never amount to anything.

And no, the teacher didn't add, 'relatively speaking' afterwards.

No doubt Hermann was so upset by the comment he rushed home at the speed of light, but to put this magnificent howler into context, at the time Albert wasn't seven, he was in his mid-teens and was soon to write his first scientific paper, *The Investigation of the State of Aether in Magnetic Fields*. How the teacher could have been so misguided in his assessment of young Albert is quite astonishing, and even though this particular pedagogue's name has been lost in the sands of time it is strongly suspected that his first name was Ernest and that the initial draft of $E = mc2$ was in fact; Ernest is a massive cock squared.

Another who can lay claim to being given a child and ever so slightly underestimating his potential was one of John Lennon's teachers who, in a school report, wrote of the young scamp that he was:

Certainly on the road to failure.

Hmm, cue Beatles/John Lennon based puns. Presumably it was a long and winding road and the teacher was just a jealous guy who'd had a hard day's night.

Enough already; suffice to say that by writing those comments John's teacher was certainly on the road to huge personal and professional embarrassment, possibly via Nottingham.

2. Shocking behaviour

Before our modern and so-called enlightened age, physical punishment was a staple of life for millions of schoolchildren. Teachers would dish out a good ear-tweaking, slippering, belting or caning at the drop of a hat, especially if the lesson was, 'Hat Holding', and, as far as the future went, there were those who looked ahead to a time when these unpleasant activities were discontinued and replaced with something that took away all the unnecessary pain and hardship they inflicted on teachers.

One such forward thinker was a children's columnist with the *Chicago Tribune* who went by the name of Uncle Richard. (Yes, it screams paedo, but just in case his descendants have grounds to sue, we're not suggesting that at all.) In 1900, as many of his kind were doing, he turned his attentions to the year 2000 and suggested that, by then, schools would be equipped with a revolutionary new piece of kit to get children to do exactly as they were instructed:

> The teachers in the schools will have wonderful instruments on their desks that will record the name of every boy that whispers and all the teacher will have to do to bring swift punishment to the malefactor will be to press a certain button on the desk, and a current of electricity will shoot through the victim, and make him think he is a human pin-cushion.

Ye Gods, if that's the punishment for whispering, one can only imagine what you'd get for chewing gum.

It's easy to scoff though and no doubt there are a fair few teachers reading Uncle Dick's words and thinking, 'if only'. Who knows, perhaps one day there'll be some sort of compromise and teachers can be armed with Taser guns, though no doubt the annoying health and safety brigade will find some reason to object.

The kindly uncle hadn't finished though and continued thusly:

> Fond parents when they wish their offsprings to arise in the morning will not have to shout up the back stairs fifteen or twenty times and finally spring that old gag about coming 'right up there now, with this apple tree switch, do you hear me?' No, indeed. The parent of the year 2000 will press a small button in the sitting-room, and the bed in which the boy is sleeping will have

convulsions, and the boy will be hurled clear across the room. An electric spanker will then do a few stunts, and the boy will be glad to make haste in attiring himself suitably for appearance in polite society.

And this, don't forget, is what *fond* parents will do; ye Gods again, so much for school days being the best of your life.

It's not known what became of Uncle Richard, but it seems likely that after leaving the *Tribune* he went on to find gainful employment as an electric chair executioner. Or perhaps he became a successful stand up comic, wowing the adoring crowds with his hilarious apple tree switch gag.

3. Lost his Elgin Marbles

While Uncle Richard seemed to have a certain sense of mistrust in relation to young people, Professor Walter B. Gunnison writing in the 30 December 1900 edition of the *Brooklyn Daily Eagle*, took a somewhat different line. Far from envisioning a future of state-sanctioned torture within educational establishments, he believed there were other ways in which today's little darlings could flourish and blossom into tomorrow's big darlings.

The school houses will be models in architecture and in sanitary arrangement and they will be filled with everything in the way of decoration and equipment that a cultured and refined taste can suggest.

Rarely can schoolchildren have been described as having, *'cultured and refined taste'*, though perhaps that is doing the young people of Brooklyn a disservice. Or maybe not. But what exactly did the good prof mean when he said that schools would be filled *'with everything in the way of decoration and equipment'*? Thankfully there is no need to speculate.

> Pictures of the best artists and models of the world's great sculp-
> tures will here have their true home. Much that is now buried in
> inaccessible museums will be transferred to the schools simply
> because there they can be most effective for good.

Yes, in complete contrast to Uncle Richard, Walter B. was so
trusting of pupils that he believed some of the globe's most
prized artefacts would eventually be kept and put on display in
their classrooms.

And indeed it would be wonderful for kids to have priceless
treasures such as the Mona Lisa and Tutankhamun's sac-
ramental death mask stored inside their classroom art cup-
board. How their faces would light up in wonderment and joy
as the teacher gets them out to allow the children unique access
to these great works. How, also, would the teacher's face contort
with hitherto un-experienced levels of agony as, egged on by
his mates, Baddiel minor draws a moustache on Mona's smiling
(or is it unsmiling?) face, and Zucker major uses the death mask
as a Frisbee.

There are very good reasons why irreplaceable artworks are
kept in secure, alarmed museums away from little chocolate-
covered hands, all of which seem to have been completely lost
on Professor Gunnison, himself a school principal at the time
(of Erasmus Hall High School). Indeed, it is tempting to posit
the question, why was he given leave to write such flights of
fancy in a respected newspaper when he should have been
managing his educational establishment?

Well, having posited the question, let us posit an answer.
Perhaps it was because, at the time, the business manager of
the *Brooklyn Daily Eagle*, was one Herbert F. Gunnison, brother
of the good professor. Who knows; suffice to say that having
made his prediction, Walter probably expected that by now it
would be buried in an inaccessible newspaper. How very wrong
he was.

4. A first class degree in getting it wrong

We turn now to our old chum Mr John Elfreth Watkins Jr and his magnificent predictions for the year 2000 made in the *Ladies Home Journal* of the year 1900.

Prediction number 17 of the 29 he lavished upon the world was entitled, 'How Children Will Be Taught', which is somewhat misleading as he focuses more on how much it will cost for children to be taught, which in his opinion is very little. Well, nothing really. Oh, and having set the prediction up to be about children, he kicks off by talking about adults.

A university education will be free to every man and woman.

Bless him, it's a wonderful aspiration, but, at a time when university tuition fees in the UK are set to treble and it can take graduates up to 25 years to pay off a student loan he couldn't have got it more wrong, unless, perhaps, he'd predicted that students would be paid to attend university if they turned up wearing gorilla outfits.

Continuing on he does milk the free thing just a little.

Poor students will be given free board, free clothing and free books if ambitious and actually unable to meet their school and college expenses.

Have you spotted the inconsistency yet? Yes, having previously said that a university education will be free to everyone, he then talks about college expenses, you don't need a GCSE in Common Sense to figure out the problem with that one.

There's also the very interesting, '*if ambitious*' comment which seems to imply that poor students will only get the freebies if they have the requisite desire to learn, something that could possibly be assessed in the following way.

University Applications Officer: 'So, how much do you want to study French?'

Poor Student: 'Oh really a lot.'

University Applications Officer: 'Really?'

Poor Student: 'Really, really.'

University Applications Officer: 'Okay, you're in.'

Finally John does actually say something about children by adding,

Etiquette and housekeeping will be important studies in the public schools.

Not entirely correct unless he was talking about the correct etiquette to use when going through a metal detector and housekeeping being how well you maintain your virtual home in some virtual internet land where the currency is called Flebacks and your avatar is reminiscent of a half-dead crow.

5. Textbook error

There's no doubting that Thomas Edison was a clever bunny. He invented loads of things like the long lasting light bulb, the phonograph (ask your parents, actually, make that grandparents) and the motion picture camera. No wonder then that when interviewed for the *Miami Metropolis* in 1911 he was described as follows: '*None but a wizard dare raise the curtain and disclose the secrets of the future; and what wizard can do it with so sure a hand as Mr Thomas Alva Edison.*'

So sure a hand, and yet so silly a middle name.

To be fair to Mr Edison he did make some predictions in that 1911 article that weren't too bad, and to be even fairer he made plenty of other predictions that became reality. And he was definitely onto something when he claimed:

I believe that the motion picture is destined to revolutionize our education system and that in a few years it will supplant largely, if not entirely the use of textbooks.

However, his idea of motion pictures revolutionising the education system involved the use of *educational* films – lectures being delivered by brilliant professors or hands-on lessons that inspired children to create and problem solve. The movies that actually supplanted the education system for older students were more like *American Pie* and computer game 'movies' like *Mortal Combat*. And for younger children, movies supplanting textbooks generally means being huddled round a crap TV at wet break time watching some tawdry Disney classic with a muffled soundtrack.

The other thing to mention of course is that Edison invented the motion picture camera so movies replacing textbooks was a bit of wishful thinking. Still, you can't blame him for trying.

6. 'You've been found guilty of handing your homework in late; six months' solitary confinement!'

To rehabilitate or to punish? Such rages the argument about prison that remains unresolved to this very day, but in 1931 America's National Education Association predicted not that it would be resolved, rather that it would become entirely redundant.

Crime will be virtually abolished by transferring to the preventive processes of the school and education the problems of conduct which police, courts, and prisons now remedy when it is too late.

Well, what a glorious future in store, one in which we can, in fact, return to the past and leave doors unlocked secure in the knowledge that all thoughts of house-burglary and petty larceny will have been remedied at school.

Surely though this utopia is a long, long way off, a distant dream even then. Well, not exactly. The prediction was included in an article entitled, 'What We Shall Be Like In 1950', giving society a mere 19 years to eradicate all crime. It's patently absurd, particularly if you consider that with good behaviour they'd probably only have 12 years. But it's not solely the time scale that borders on the ludicrous. There's the small matter of precisely what these preventative processes were and how exactly teachers were going to implement them. Presumably, they'd have to learn a whole range of new skills.

TEACHERS REQUIRED FOR NEW NURSERY SCHOOL

SUCCESSFUL APPLICANTS SHOULD BE PROFICIENT IN:

- Use of long and short handed batons
- Securing pupils in leg irons
- Riot control
- Hitting without leaving bruises
- Handcuffing

So here we are in the 21st century and crime rates are soaring. Noble though it was, clearly they were aiming too high in the 1930s and today it would be a start if we could just abolish the criminal activities that actually go on *in* schools.

7. Late bloomers

When should children start going to school? It's a question that has vexed educationalists since the dawn of time. Five, six or if the parents are really exhausted, maybe three months old.

Even today no one knows for sure, which makes it all the more curious that back in 1937 a teacher from Columbia University thought he had the answer.

> By the year 2000, we won't send children to school until they are 10 years old.

Yup, even if they really want to go, we won't let them. So what will they do instead? Our brilliant teacher had the answer.

> While they are young, we will keep them busy building healthy bodies in the fresh air.

And you know what? That teacher had the right idea. Staying away from school until you're ten and building a healthy body in the fresh air is a pretty spot-on aspiration. If only someone had listened to him, taken heed of his suggestion and made it an international law.

Unfortunately, it seems that children are starting school earlier and earlier and taking tests and exams at ever younger ages. As for the fresh air bit, it was just a distant dream. If this particular predictor had wanted to be accurate he should have said that by the year 2000, 'children will spend vast tracts of their time in heavily fuggy rooms, playing violent video games while building obese bodies'.

8. Fight! Fight! Fight! Fight! Fight!

> War, uh, yeah … what is it good for? Absolutely nothing, say it again.

So sang Edwin Starr back in 1970, and it's a very fair contention. However, turn the clock back 31 years to 1939 and it's quite possible that the lyrics might have gone something like this:

'War, uh, yeah ... what is it good for? Overhauling the entire education system, say it again.'

Yes, with the world on the brink of war those canny publishers at The Greystone Press saw a golden opportunity and rushed out a book entitled, *What Will Happen and What To Do When War Comes*. It was authored by a number of respected types and no doubt contained plenty of sage advice such as, 'you'll die' and 'make sure your will is up to date', along with some very interesting predictions about education made by one W.W. Chaplin.

For example,

> The birth of war will be the death of education as we have known it. 'Useless' subjects, which will mean everything that does not train for war, will gradually be dropped from the curricula.

It's a bold statement and one that, had it been correct might have seen school timetables as follows:

	Monday	Tuesday	Wednesday	Thursday	Friday
9.00 – 10.00	Killing with guns	Impregnating local women	Standing to attention	Standing to attention	Pillage
10.00 – 11.00	Killing with grenades	Sexually transmitted diseases	Marching	Looting	Escaping P.O.W. camps
11.00 – 12.00	Killing with bare hands	Care for the wounded	Pitching camp	Surrender	Dying with dignity
Lunch - powdered egg					
1.00 – 2.00	Surrender	Pillage	Dying with dignity	Killing with bare hands	Impregnating local women
2.00 – 3.00	Escaping P.O.W. camps	Looting	Dying without dignity	Killing with grenades	Sexually transmitted diseases

It's a great timetable of lessons and no doubt schoolchildren everywhere rejoiced at the prospect, but even though over time highly-trained military nations would emerge, there is one small problem; none of their subjects would be able to read. Or write. Or add up. Or be able to dissect a frog. None of which really matters that much, until, that is, you're on the road to Dunkirk and incorrectly read the signs along the way, leading to the invasion of Dunstable.

Special mention must also go to the rarely seen, but correct plural of curriculum, curricula. Clearly Mr Chaplin himself wasn't educated during a time of war.

Brilliantly, to top off Mr Chaplin's prediction, he made the following claim:

> All liberal books, all books giving 'the other side of the question' will be banned and very likely burned as they have been in other countries. A book like this would be the first to go.

Well, there's liberal and there's liberal, but calling a book that suggest schools give up teaching anything that doesn't train for war liberal is stretching the definition to breaking point.

Perhaps though his reasoning for writing that last prediction was slightly more canny and in fact he'd hoped people would grab a copy of his book from the local bookstore before it ended up singeing nicely on an open fire at some outdoor, bloodthirsty, gun-toting war celebration.

Well, all's fair in love, war and publishing.

9. Invasion of the Teachers

There's always going to be a need for teachers, which, you'd have thought, would in some way be related to the number of pupils. The more pupils there are, the more teachers there are; it's a simple equation. Not so according to business entrepreneur Roger W. Babson who, in his 1940s tome, *Looking Ahead Fifty Years*, wrote,

As I visualise the next fifty years I see the number of teachers increase as the number of agriculturalists, skilled labourers and industrial workers decrease.

Clearly there's something far more complex going on here, though perhaps only in Roger's head.

However, it's a lovely thought. Class sizes would decrease dramatically until every child had their own personal teacher. A great education would be had by all, with only one problem; there'd be no jobs at the end of it, other than teaching.

Sorry Mr Babson, your prediction is about as successful as your attempt to become President of the United States, something he did in 1940 as the chosen candidate of The Prohibition Party. He polled a whopping 0.1 per cent of the vote, narrowly losing out to Franklin D. Roosevelt who polled 54.7 per cent. Maybe, in this instance, the number of votes decreased as the number of stupid predictions increased.

10. Walls have ears, and big words written on them

David Sarnoff was quite a player. He was a very successful American businessman at the helm of radio and television in the 1920s and beyond, founding the National Broadcasting Corporation (NBC) and running the Radio Corporation of America (RCA).

Consequently he made a fair few predictions about telly and radio, most of which were rather shrewd, but when he turned his attentions to education he came just a little unstuck, as with the following, which was reported in the *Chicago Tribune* of 1959.

Another pushbutton development will be projection of microfilm books on the ceiling or wall in large type. To increase their impact on students, an electronic voice may accompany the visual passages.

So education as a sort of planetarium then, with kids craning their necks to read the latest worksheet projected onto the ceiling. The amount of wall space for even the shortest textbook would be prohibitive it seems, unless all schools were moved to The Great Wall of China, in which case kids would be able to read a great deal, though only if they had a decent pair of walking boots.

There's also this possibility of an electronic voice to increase the impact on students, but what impact exactly? Get a sinister, terrifying Christopher Lee style voice and the impact would be to scare the students shitless, which, come to think of it, might not be a bad thing for the little bastards.

11. *Complete and utter rubbish, you're in detention*

There's nothing like a world's fair to give prediction junkies a massive fix of the good stuff and back in 1962 the venue for plenty of futuristic fun and games was, of course, Seattle, where the event was also known as the Century 21 Exposition. It was looking ahead 40 years to the way off future of 2002 and, if you weren't excited enough at the prospect, the fair's official programme was sure to have even the most pessimistic of visitor tingling with anticipation.

'What time is it?' asks a young voice. From somewhere overhead comes the answer: 'It is now ... and again. Today and tomorrow's today. It is your time, child of the ever-present future.'

Yes, out damn cynic and let your heart be melted by the wonderment to behold.

The programme notes continue in a similar vein of gooey loveliness until we reach the following.

You hear a little girl's voice. 'Why? Where? What for? There's so much I want to know about yesterday, today and tomorrow.'

Well, little girl, why, where and what for might be tricky to answer, but we can tell you this.

> Now you are in a school of tomorrow ... its walls made of jets of air, its tables standing on invisible legs, its floating canvas roof controlled to catch the sun. Memory-retention machines whir in the background. Television screens mirror the day's lessons.

Whoa there, this needs some serious consideration. Walls made of jets of air? Not the easiest to put displays up on, even with Blu-Tack. And how exactly children are meant to concentrate on what the teacher is droning on about when there's a fantastic levitation and body boarding wave mere centimetres away, is anyone's guess.

It really is an incredible notion, though it would have the benefit of allowing schools not to waste money on expensive drying machines in the toilets. Pupils could just stick their hands in the jets of air to dry off, though care would be needed not to put your hand right through the wall in case you disturb next door's lesson or punch a student working in the adjacent classroom on the side of the head.

Then we have the truly wonderful prediction that tables would stand on invisible legs, their own presumably. So, after years of intensive research scientists finally unlock the secret of invisibility, but they're only going to use it on table legs in schools. Seems unlikely, but to borrow one of the little girl's questions, er why? Isn't it more annoying not to be able to see the legs? If you really wanted to improve children's education surely the thing to do would be to make the teacher invisible; they'd have no idea where he or she was and have no option but to get on with their work.

Continuing the disbelief, we now come to the school's floating canvas roof controlled to catch the sun. Well, of course, it would have to be floating because the walls are jets of air, though it's always possible that the roof could be kept aloft by invisible supports. Given the scale of insanity here, it's tempting to wonder whether by, catch the sun, they actually meant, literally catch the sun in case it should plummet to earth, but even by the standards of this prediction, that seems unlikely.

Finally we come to the memory retention machines whirring in the background – well, only if someone remembers to turn them on – and the television screens that mirror the lessons so that, presumably, children can watch themselves being taught and see the teacher throwing the invisible blackboard cleaner at them and shouting, 'Oi, face the front', something that wouldn't be necessary if there weren't any television screens in the first place.

12. Stop wanking at the back

Topping the Century 21 Exposition's barking mad prediction takes some doing, but it's just possible Billy Rojas, a man described as, '*a pioneer in academic future studies*', has done it. Billy was a contributor to a 1972 book called *Futures Conditional*, described online as, 'currently unavailable', which contained essays and such like from noted futurists of the time.

Billy's entry fell very much into the 'suchlike' category as, rather than an essay, he presented a chronologically ordered list of newspaper headlines that he claimed we could expect to see in the near future. Many were both strange and strangely specific such as his headline for November 1973 which read,

Stones break up. New music stirs U.S.; Cheyenne native rock-and-tom-tom group tops charts.

Or this from June 1975,

Electro-pop, completely synthetic beverage starts a new food craze: Electro-snax, Electro-suppers are marketed.

You get the measure of the man.

What concerns us here though is a particular headline Billy predicted would appear in October 1977.

Sexual intercourse allowed in Yale sex. ed classes. Harvard follows suit.

It's a headline that many students at these prestigious colleges would no doubt dearly love to see, but before we let their over-excitement run away with them, it's only fair that we point out the numerous ambiguities within it.

Did Mr Rojas mean only that demonstrations of sexual inter-course would be allowed in a way imagined, albeit comically, by Monty Python's John Cleese in *The Meaning of Life*? In this instance only the teacher and a colleague could have sex while the students looked on, bored to tears. Or perhaps he meant that, having been taught the basics, the students themselves would be allowed to practise what they'd learnt on each other. An intriguing prospect, particularly if they moved on to group work, though a lot would depend on the teacher's pairings.

'I don't care if he does have terrible acne, dandruff and hasn't washed for three weeks, if you don't have sex with him Sandra, I'll have no alternative but to put you in detention.'

Then there is the possibility that students, fed up studying the reproductive organs of the common toad, could simply amuse themselves by shagging, a school rule that could easily transfer to other subjects; in which case, it's highly unlikely anyone would be paying attention in double physics.

The possibilities really are both endless and mind-boggling such as parents' evening; 'I'm afraid your daughter really does need to work on her blowjobs Mr and Mrs Lewinsky'. And, 'That bell is for me. No one is leaving until all the used condoms have been tidied away'.

But, having predicted the headlines, Billy-boy Rojas proves himself to be a confident fellow by stating that the events will, probably happen – in some cases undoubtedly happen – although not necessarily in the order presented.

It's a truly great get-out clause which completely sidesteps one of the fundamental aspects of being a futurist, that of saying when your predictions will happen. Any idiot can say, 'space-ships will land on Mars one day', but it takes a very special kind of idiot to say, 'students will be allowed to have sex in sex education classes in October 1977, though actually it might not be then, it might be before or after'.

Billy it would seem though, just can't help himself and if the rug needed to be pulled further out from beneath him, he obliged in 1976 by saying,

> Forecasting the future is now in about the same shape as fore-casting the weather was before the United States Weather Bureau. It's disorganized. There's no set of standards that everybody goes by. I'd say it will be ten or fifteen years before future forecasting is validated.

Of course Billy, and that will probably, nay undoubtedly happen, though maybe some time sooner or perhaps later.

13. Come on, get out of bed, it's time to get ready for home

A brace of predictions now, both of which fundamentally miss the whole point of school, which, as we all know, is to provide somewhere kids can go to while their parents work or relax.

The first comes from a 1981 book entitled, *School, Work and Play (World of Tomorrow)* which, under the heading, 'Homework of the Future', begins reassuringly with;

> In the near future it's likely that children will still go to school and there will be human teachers, much as happens now.

Well that's a relief; those supply teachers from Saturn can be very nasty. However, there is a shock in store.

> ... if we look further into the future, there could be no schools and no teachers. Schoolwork may not exist. Instead you will have to do homework, for you will learn everything at home using your home video computer. You'll learn a wide range of subjects quickly and at a time of day to suit you. However, it's probable that someone like a teacher will visit your home to check that all is going well.

It's just so wonderfully innocent and naïve whereas the reality is so horribly evil and unpleasant. Would that the teacher was only dropping by to check that you were getting on with your studies and not, as would be the case today, that you were playing nasty computer games, looking at porn, hacking into someone else's bank account, using your Mum's credit card to buy stuff from Amazon, downloading music and films, Facebooking your mates, Skyping your mates and looking at more porn.

Then there is the suggestion that learning at home on the computer would enable you to learn quickly. Well it might if you just accept the information parrot fashion which, given that Wikipedia once stated that David Beckham was a Chinese goalkeeper from the 18th century and Robbie Williams earns money eating hamsters, might not be such a great idea. It could take a while for the occasional community teacher to sort that lot out, especially if the time of day that suits your learning style is four in the morning.

Clearly a more sedate approach was needed and the following year it was duly provided in, *Encounters with the Future: A Forecast of Life into the 21st Century.*

> By 1990 the (television) cable will touch all parts of human life:
> It will allow students to attend school three days a week, letting

them learn at home on the other days over the two-way television.

Leaving aside for one moment the fact that 1990 is some small matter of ten years short of the 21st century, parents will be relieved to hear that they can still offload the kids for three days a week. As for the other two days, it seems these would be spent at home sitting in front of the telly, thus not really distinguishing them from the weekend, apart from the fact that, one presumes, a teacher would be at the other end of these two-way tellies, giving a lesson.

It's not a bad idea not least because schools could have adverts in between lessons: 'Coming up, it's Maths where this week Mr Jones will be teaching Calculus, but first, no, not compare the meerkat.com, it's compare the market.com.'

There's also the additional issue that, in order to throw a sicky, you'd have to look shit as well as sound it.

In fact, to save on energy the pupils could all go round to one person's house and watch the lesson together. Better still, they could all go round to the teacher's house and have the lesson there, though it might be something of a trek to get to another teacher's house for the next lesson, so perhaps all the teachers could come together in one big building and the pupils could congregate there for lessons. It's a bit of a ridiculous prediction, but you never know.

SCIENCE AND TECHNOLOGY

Science or technology, technology or science, what came first? It's very much a chicken and egg situation. Only, at the same time, it very much isn't. Clearly the science has to come first and then the technology, based on that science, follows.

It's incredible to think that that question has been vexing people for so many years, but then it's also incredible that an area in which nothing is said with any degree of certainty before a hypothesis has been proposed and then rigorously tested and re-tested until it has been proved beyond doubt, is littered with bold statements of 'fact' that are based on the unscientific musings of what you might reasonably assume are pseudo-scientific wackjobs.

Remarkably, however, many of the predictions that follow have not been made by that highly specialised branch of scientist known as mad, but by some of the greatest minds that have ever existed. Perhaps it's worth proposing a hypothesis that states: when asked to predict the future eminent scientists take leave of their senses and say any old bollocks. A government funding grant in the region of £10 million should be enough to research this burning question.

As for technology, it seems while great progress and advances are being made in this field, much less is being made when it comes to pronouncements about the viability of new technology and how it is going to transform our lives. Broadly, these pronouncements fall into two categories; those who predict it'll never work and those who predict it'll work too well.

The effect for us lesser minds though is troubling. We put our faith in these men and women of science, so if one of them was to say, 'the toaster will never catch on', naturally the last thing we'd go and do is rush out and buy one, thus missing out on lots of lovely, buttery toast, possibly with jam.

The answer, of course, is for science to lay the groundwork for the greatest technological advance of them all; the invention of the bullshit detector, a product that were it to work, should immediately be put to use on all those who would doubtlessly come out and predict that it would never work.

1. What's the point?

The boundaries of science are limitless, or that's the theory at least. The quest for knowledge should be neverending as discoveries open doors to yet more discoveries and so it goes on.

Begging to differ would be one Simon Cameron, an American senator who, in 1861, took it upon himself to try and close those doors by saying,

> I am tired of all this thing called science. . . . We have spent millions in that sort of thing for the last few years, and it is time it should be stopped.

As well as more generally predicting the end of science – well, the end of *this thing* called science – specifically Senator Cameron was calling for the end of funding to research at an education centre, The Smithsonian Institute. It might gall him somewhat to know that the Institute is still going and in 2011 requested $796.7 million from the US government.

Another who pushed the door closed, but then decided to leave it open a teeny bit was physicist Albert Abraham Michelson. Michelson was certainly no slouch. In 1907 he became the first American to win a Nobel Prize in any of the sciences, but back in 1894 he was a prime candidate for the Nobel Prize in 'oh dear, I wish I hadn't said that', when he told anyone who would listen that,

> The more important fundamental laws and facts of physical science have all been discovered, and these are now so firmly established that the possibility of their ever being supplanted in consequence of new discoveries is exceedingly remote. ... Our future discoveries must be looked for in the sixth place of decimals.

He was given a 0.000001 chance of being right.

Michelson wasn't alone though. Echoing him, was British scientist Lord Kelvin, after whom the Kelvin scale of temperature measurement is named, who in 1900 told the world that,

> There is nothing new to be discovered in physics now; all that remains is more and more precise measurement.

This was in a speech to the British Association for the Advancement of Science.

A year later and the *Washington Post* decided to get in on the act by making this rather remarkable statement in an editorial.

> We have sanitation, surgery, drainage, plumbing – every product of science and accessory to luxury. It seems impossible to imagine any improvement on what we have.

Well, there's impossible and there's impossible, but surely the good folk at the *Washington Post* could have stretched the limits of their combined imaginations ever so slightly and come up with the odd improvement or two. It seems not, though apparently their current offices do have extremely good plumbing, which more than makes up for the lack of heating, air conditioning or computers.

2. This is the point

While some were intent on closing doors, others were opening them and charging on through at an alarming rate such that they didn't really stop to check what was written on them, which in most cases was, 'Do Not Enter.'

One such door freak was 19th century French physiologist Claude Bernard who has been described as, *'one of the greatest of all men of science'*, an outstanding tribute indeed and one that neatly sidesteps this little prediction he made in 1869.

> (One hundred years hence) ... man will be so completely the master of organic law that he would create life in competition with God.

No doubt God was quaking in his celestial booties (if you believe in God), but come 1969 Frankenstein failed to materialise and the Lord could at last relax a little.

Next through the doors of embarrassment was Alfred Russel Wallace a man who goes a long way to proving that for every Bob Geldof there's a Midge Ure. You see, Alf is considered to be the co-discoverer of the theory of evolution, but frankly, who knew? Very few, that's for certain, which may have something to do with the following prediction he blurted out in 1899,

> In the coming century, Phrenology will assuredly attain general importance. It will prove itself to be the true science of mind. Its practical uses in education, in self-discipline, in the reformatory

treatment of criminals and in the remedial treatment of the insane will give it one of the highest places in the hierarchy of the sciences.

Phrenology, for those who might not know (yes, we had no idea until we looked it up), is the linking of bumps on the head to personality traits and is termed a pseudoscience much like Homeopathy and, for some pseudo-intelligent people, Evolution itself. Far from being of general importance, it's now of no importance whatsoever and one can only assume that, clever as Alfie was, he must have had a missing link or two in that otherwise first class mind.

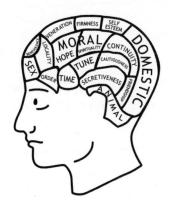 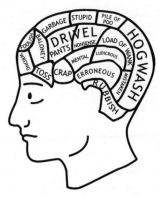

Phrenology as it was   Phrenology as it is today

3. Not particularly inventive

According to Galileo, *'doubt is the father of invention'*, so clearly it's married to necessity and its offspring spend their lives desperately needing to do things but being hampered by uncertainty. For many however, though they may doubt inventions or the future of inventions, they have no doubt about their doubt, undoubtedly.

Way back in Roman times, around AD 73, Britain was governed by a chap called Sextus Julius Frontinus. He was a pretty bright spark having received respect for his authoritative writings on the aqueducts of Rome, but when he penned one of his follow ups, *Strategemata*, a lot of that respect, unlike the aqueducts, dried up, quite possibly because of this commentus maximus.

> I lay aside all ideas of any new works or engines of war, the invention of which long-ago reached its limit, and in which I see no hope for further improvement . . . .

Apparently when word got back to Emperor Vespasianus in Rome he was heard to utter, 'oh no, not et tu Sextus'.

A few hundred years later and we find ourselves back with Lord Kelvin again who, in 1883 when president of The Royal Society, a posh club for scientists, stood before his peers and bellowed,

> X-Rays will prove to be a hoax.

Tempting as it is to say that there were plenty who saw through his prediction, it's only fair to point out that three years later when the boy Kelvin was shown evidence that x-rays worked, he, very magnanimously and graciously, accepted that they worked.

For every Doubting Thomas though, there's a Cocksure Lionel prepared to claim the earth for their invention, which is almost literally what another Nobel Prize winner, Herbert Simon did in 1965. Herbie won his prize for Economics, but he juggled an awful lot of hats, one of which was the Stetson of Artificial Intelligence, a field in which he is regarded as a pioneer. Although given the following prediction it's possible that the specific branch of A.I. that he was a pioneer in was ludicrous over-hyping.

> By 1985 machines will be capable of doing any work Man can do.

Clearly Herb had got a little carried away, especially when you consider that over 45 years later we still haven't got a machine that can cook up a perfect Spanish omelette, while putting three kids to bed and speaking in depth to Aunt Sandra about her stocks and shares portfolio.

A couple of years on and French nuclear physicist and chemical engineer, Jacques Bergier, someone whose intelligence was supposedly real, said the following about 1984:

> ... there will be thousands of appliances similar to those of today: vacuum cleaners, electric drills, toasters, irons and so on.

It's brilliant, the man was clearly a genius. Oh wait a second, there's more. He then went on to say,

> But they will be enormously different in one respect. They will no longer need to be plugged into the electric current, but will be driven instead by an independent source of energy.

Well, there are batteries and cordless robot vacuum cleaners and duster busters, but most appliances are still plugged into the electric current and it looks as if it will remain that way for some time to come.

Technological advancement and invention owes a lot to learning from the mistakes of the past though, which is more than can be said for some people who just can't help falling into that old trap of completely writing off a product that goes on to be a world conqueror.

One such person was Lord Sir Duke King Alan Sugar, businessman, entrepreneur, telly host and Sid James look-alike who, in 2005, saw fit to make the following claim about the latest new invention flooding the market;

Next Christmas the iPod will be dead, finished, gone, kaput.

Al, with very little regret, you're fired.

4. Let there be light

In 1878 Paris staged its third World's Fair, or Exposition Universelle as they insisted on calling it for some reason. It was a big success attracting millions of visitors, many of whom, no doubt, marvelled at the electric lights that lit up the Avenue de l'Opéra and the Place de l'Opéra. This impressive display probably prompted many to think, 'Hello, I reckon there might well be something in this electric light thing', only in French, unless they were foreign visitors in which case they would, more likely than not, have thought it in their own languages.

English surgeon and dermatologist Sir Erasmus Wilson had a rather different opinion exemplified in this quip he made.

When the Paris Exhibition closes electric light will close with it and no more be heard of.

It's possible Erasmus could try and squirm out of it by claiming that he simply meant once the exhibition was over, they'd turn the lights off, but it's unlikely he'd get away with it. It's also possible that he was being paid to talk down electric lighting by either the candle or the gas light industry fearful at the prospect of lost business.

The following year, 1879, Thomas Edison gave the first demonstration of his incandescent light bulb, an event which also provided him with the opportunity to give an early demonstration of the 'soundbite'. *'We will make electricity so cheap that only the rich will burn candles.'* There's no record of how the poor responded though some claim they did so with their own soundbite, telling Edison exactly where he could shove those candles.

Needless to say, it wasn't long before Edison's achievement was being decried. First up was engineer and inventor Sir William Siemens who on hearing about the light bulb said,

> Such startling announcements as these should be deprecated as being unworthy of science and mischievous to its true progress.

Next to wade in was president of America's Stevens Institute of Technology, Henry Morton, who said,

> Everyone acquainted with the subject will recognize it as a conspicuous failure.

So Edison clearly earned the bragging rights on that one, but a few years later, in 1889, he lost them entirely when commenting on another new invention, not a million miles from his own.

> Fooling around with alternating current is just a waste of time. Nobody will use it, ever.

All of two years later, what is described as being the, *'first truly modern power station'*, opened its doors to the world. It supplied high voltage AC power. Edison falls into that special camp of inventors whose successful ideas are ridiculed and who ridicule the successful ideas of others. Psychotherapists would have had a field day with his mind.

Perhaps the last to enlighten us on this matter should be British geneticist J.B.S. Haldane who, in 1923, told The Heretics at Cambridge University that,

> It is a fairly safe prophecy that in 50 years light will cost about a
> fiftieth of its present price, and there will be no more night in our
> cities.

Presumably then, for a good night's sleep, we'll all need to move to the country.

5. Is that a machine gun in your pocket?

Sir Hiram Stevens Maxim has a long list of inventions to his name; the mousetrap, curling iron, a coffee substitute and a pocket menthol inhaler to name a few. The one that blows all the others away though is undoubtedly the Maxim Gun, or, to give it its more familiar name, the Machine Gun.

Hiram patented the gun in 1884 and its effect was immediate. Suddenly, young boys could run around making a gun with their fingers and fire repeatedly without reloading, instead of just once.

While warmongers everywhere might have been whooping in delight, peacemongers weren't quite so enchanted by this new piece of weaponry, which is possibly why in 1893, British physician and psychologist Havelock Ellis posed this little poser to Maxim.

> Will this gun not make war more terrible?

It's a fair question, but Maxim had the answer.

> No, it will make war impossible.

And of course he was right, there hasn't been a war since. (Curiously, Havelock means 'sea war', so perhaps subconsciously Maxim was hoping to make Havelock impossible.)

In 1910 people were still grumbling on about Maxim's harmless little toy, so much so that the French Director General of Infantry was moved to tell the French Parliament the following.

> Make no mistake, this weapon will change absolutely nothing.

Well, after World War One we can only presume that it changed his mind at the very least.

By 1937 the efficacy of the machine gun as a killing machine can have been in little doubt. Nonetheless, writing in *The Road To Wigan Pier*, brilliant journalist, writer and oft successful visionary, George Orwell, was moved to make the following prediction:

> We may find in the long run that tinned food is a deadlier weapon than the machine-gun.

We may indeed, but only if someone is able to repeatedly and accurately throw tins very rapidly into a large crowd of people.

6. A lot of fuss about a lot

While the machine gun might have excited fans of mass killing for a short time, it soon became passé, leaving quite a considerable gap in the total annihilation market.

Attempts to fill this focused on the atom, admittedly not only for destruction, but also for energy, though as by-products go, blowing up the world is quite a big one.

If the public were worried at the prospect, they needn't have been because there was a veritable stampede of highly learned types on hand to reassure them, such as Nobel Laureate, Robert Millikan. Here's what he had to say in 1928.

> There is no likelihood that man can ever tap the power of the atom. The glib supposition of utilizing atomic energy when our

coal has run out is a completely unscientific Utopian dream, a childish bug-a-boo.

Floyd W. Parsons was slightly less of an authority being just an engineer and magazine editor with no known prizes to his name (though he might well have won some at school). Consequently, he needed to go big with his pronouncement.

Nothing is gained by exaggerating the possibilities of tomorrow. We need not worry over the consequences of breaking up the atom.

With Floyd's words arguably falling on deaf ears, it was time to bring out the really big guns, the top boys, and in physics at the time it didn't get any bigger than Bertie and Ernie, Einstein and Rutherford.

Here are Albert's thoughts on the matter in 1932:

There is not the slightest indication that (nuclear energy) will ever be obtainable. It would mean that the atom would have to be shattered at will.

And here are Ernest's the following year.

The energy produced by the breaking down of the atom is a very poor kind of thing. Anyone who expects a source of power from the transformation of these atoms is talking moonshine.

Heartening as it is to anyone of limited intelligence to discover that two of the world's foremost genii can get things so wrong, it is also a little worrying. Who should the public turn to? Who should they listen to about matters of great import? Should it be great political leaders? Well no, not if this 1939 prediction by none other than Winston Churchill is anything to go by.

Atomic energy might be as good as our present-day explosives, but it is unlikely to produce anything very much more dangerous.

There's one for the pre-war spin doctors to conjure with. No doubt they'd focus in on the exact definition of 'much more dangerous', and claim that according to statistics, the actual degree of difference in the power of the explosions is not that great, though those stats would probably have been produced by Einstein and Rutherford.

Six years later and the world stood on the brink of witnessing the most deadly display of explosive weaponry in its history. If ever there was a moment for the public to need reassurance this was it. Step forward Admiral William Leahy.

The bomb will never go off, and I speak as an expert in explosives.

That was his advice to American President Truman who listened to it and decided to completely ignore it, bombing the shit out of Hiroshima and Nagasaki.

Will never happen according to explosive experts.

7. We shall eat them on the beaches

Having mentioned Winston Churchill it seems wrong not to consider another of his predictions concerning a great technological advance in the agricultural/zoological sciences. Clearly a man of refined culinary habits, when it came to eating poultry he, like many others, had his favourite part of the animal and frankly, didn't see why he should bother with the rest of it. Indeed, he looked forward to a future when his life would be rid of that particular affliction.

> 50 years hence … we shall escape the absurdity of growing a whole chicken in order to eat the breast or wing by growing these parts separately under a suitable medium.

That was in a 1931 article he wrote for *Strand* magazine, which later found its way into *Popular Mechanics* and latterly, of course, into this publication.

It is of course absurd to grow an entire chicken just to eat the breast or wing, though obviously it's perfectly acceptable to grow one solely for the legs.

Extending Churchill's prediction one must presume that he foresaw continued specialisation within this particular agricultural field such that farmers would call themselves poultry breast farmers and poultry wing farmers.

8. It doesn't compute

Computers today are as common as computers were yesterday, but incredible as it may seem, once upon a time very few people had one. In 1941 that number was exactly one because the first programmable fully automatic computing machine, the Zuse Z3, had only just been invented. No one saw fit to programme it to work out the accuracy of future predictions about computing, though if they had and it had been functioning correctly the answer old Zusey would have given would surely have been, 'not very accurate'.

The first to upset the computing applecart may or may not have been Thomas Watson who in 1943 when chairman of IBM, may or may not have said,

I think there is a world market for maybe five computers.

This oft quoted quote is the subject of much conjecture and might simply be an urban myth, though given the size of computers in those days, it's possible that if Thomas did say it, what he actually meant was that there wouldn't be enough room on the planet for more than five computers.

The real origin of the quote, or misquote, might have come from Cambridge professor Douglas Hartree who in 1951 made the following prediction. He said that in his opinion all the calculations that would ever be needed in Britain could be done on the three digital computers that were being built at the time. Apparently,

No one else would ever need machines of their own, or would be able to afford to buy them.

Quite possibly a marvellous game of Chinese whispers has gone on, and the chances are that the first statement was made in 1911 when a lowly lab assistant at Oxford University actually said, 'I bought a lovely pewter vase down the market, maybe the loveliest pewter vase in the world.'

What there is little doubt about, as has already been mentioned, is that back in the early days computers were big old beasts taking up a lot of space. Luckily, according to a March 1949 edition of *Popular Mechanics* magazine, people could look forward to a time when they were far more manageable.

Where a calculator on the ENIAC [Electronic Numerical Integrator

And Computer] is equipped with 19,000 vacuum tubes and weighs 30 tons, computers in the future may have only 1,000 vacuum tubes and perhaps only weigh 1.5 tons.

Notice that they've been somewhat canny by saying that perhaps computers will only weigh 1.5 tons, clearly they were only considering the market in laptops for giants.

While the folk at *Popular Mechanics* saw some sort of future for the computer, albeit quite a weighty one, genius mathematician John von Neumann wasn't quite so convinced.

It would appear we have reached the limits of what it is possible to achieve with computer technology ...

He made this statement in the same year, 1949, and after careful calculation added:

... although one should be careful with such statements, they tend to sound pretty silly in five years.

And in 10, 20, 30, 40, 50 and 60 years.

Thankfully the limits of computer technology had not been reached and they continued their relentless march onwards and upwards, their tentacles spreading into such areas as publishing, where the rush was on to capture the growing interest by getting books on the subject out to the general public.

One manuscript that landed on the desk of an editor at educational publisher Prentice Hall in 1957 concerned the science behind data processing. Now it's quite possible that it was badly written, dull or simply lacked consumer appeal, however that wasn't the reason given for turning it down. Here's a paragraph:

I have traveled the length and breadth of this country and talked with the best people, and I can assure you that data processing is a fad that won't last out the year.

All that effort and all that travelling just to look like a complete knobhead. Perhaps the people he spoke to were actually the best con merchants, though apart from anything else, even if the editor genuinely believed that data processing was just a passing fad, why not get the book out pronto and cash in while lesser mortals still thought it could be a possibility in an imagined future?

Two conflicting statements now, both from the same source and both from the same year. The source is the *Wall Street Journal* and the year is 1966, or vice versa. Here's what reporter Stanley Penn had to say about computers.

Despite the trends to compactness and lower costs, it is unlikely everyone will have their own computer any time soon.

Not everyone got one but a hell of a lot did. It was a misjudgement and one that he must have left off his resumé, as the following year Stan won the Pulitzer Prize.

With one of its star reporters predicting small things for small computers, it's surprising that the following also appeared in the *Journal* in 1966.

Computers are multiplying at a rapid rate. By the turn of the century there will be 220,000 in the US.

Roughly speaking they were out by multiple of a thousand. Or put another way their prediction was about one thousandth of the actual number. Curiously, whoever wrote that doesn't seem to have won a Pulitzer Prize.

Returning to the size issue again – obviously, in this case, it is important – in 1970 British physicist Desmond King-Hele brought out a book entitled, *The End of the Twentieth Century?*

The question mark is a marvellously crafty move, allowing him to squirm out of any erroneous predictions he might make, but we're not going to let him get away with that. Here's what he had to say about computers.

> Computers will benefit even more than telephones from the development of integrated circuits in ever smaller 'chips,' and very small computers may emerge.

Wonderful, question mark or no question mark, you are a genius Desmond, whatever you do, don't say anything else. OK, what else have you got?

> Most computers will probably still occupy a large room, however, because of the space needed for the ancillary software – the tapes and cards to be fed in, the operating staff, and the huge piles of paper for printing out the results. But future computers, though no smaller, will be capable of doing far more than their predecessors.

He was so near with this curiously half right, half complete and utter pants prediction. What's more he really needs to sort out his definition of, 'very small' which at the moment seems to be, massive.

By 1977, both Apple and Microsoft were up and running and no one was designating the largest room in the house to any of their products, but they didn't have things all to themselves. Also doing good business was a company called Digital Equipment Corporation run by Ken Olsen, a one time idol of Bill Gates' apparently, though that idolisation may have come to an abrupt end after Ken made this little pronouncement.

> There is no need for any individual to have a computer in his home.

It's a bold statement and one that immediately started doing the rounds, increasingly so as more and more individuals began having computers in their homes.

So what does Ken do? Well, he trots out the old, 'it's been taken out of context' line claiming that what he was talking about was the sort of computer imagined back in the earlier part of the 20th century, one that controlled everything in the house – the lights, the entertainment, the food, the temperature and so on.

So Ken, forgive us for taking you out of context but next time may be you'll be a little bit clearer.

9. Identically hopeless

In 1978 when Peter Cook uttered the immortal words, 'Dolly, will you get a Polaroid of that', it's highly unlikely that the Dolly he was referring to was a cloned sheep, primarily because at the time Dolly wasn't even a twinkle in her scientist's petri dish.

However, if at some later stage Cook had wanted to re-record those words so that they did refer to a cloned animal he might have been put off by the following.

The cloning of mammals by simple nuclear transfer is biologically impossible.

So wrote research scientists Dr James McGrath and Dr Davor Solter in a December 1984 issue of *Science*, an eminent journal and one in which you really don't want to make huge claims unless you're absolutely certain. James and Davor made the statement after deciding that there was nothing wrong with the experiments they'd been doing, hence the only possible explanation for their failure was that cloning must be impossible.

They had their supporters though, such as developmental

biologist Michael A. Frohman who in 1993 wrote a piece entitled, 'The Limits of Genetic Engineering' in which he said,

> Research during the last five years has demonstrated that cloning mammals (including humans) is theoretically impossible with today's technology – and with any technology realistically in sight.

Well he kind of had to say something like that didn't he? There's no point writing an article with that title which just says, 'there are none', that's not going to fill many column inches. Three years later Dolly the cloned sheep appeared, a development that many believe occured solely to prove the above scientists wrong.

10. The Misinformation Super Highway

On 27 January 2011 technology and market research company Forrester Research made the following prediction.

> ... online retail sales in the U.S. will increase 11.98% this year compared with 2010, to $197.3 billion from $176.2 billion.

The company also predicted similar growth in Western Europe saying online sales would rise 13.10 per cent to 91.90 Euro.

Neither of these are hopeless predictions, far from it. However, this is.

> No computer network with pretty graphics can ever replace the salespeople that make our society work.

As is this.

> Visionaries see a future of telecommuting workers, interactive libraries and multimedia classrooms. They speak of electronic

town meetings and virtual communities. Commerce and business will shift from offices and malls to networks and modems. And the freedom of digital networks will make government more democratic. Baloney. Do our computer pundits lack all common sense? The truth is no online database will replace your daily newspaper, no CD-ROM can take the place of a competent teacher and no computer network will change the way government works.

Both were made in 1995 by American astronomer and author Clifford Stoll, the first in his book *Silicon Snake Oil* and the second in an article for *Newsweek* entitled, 'The Internet? Bah!' At the time his book was pretty well received, with the *Washington Post* saying,

> *Snake Oil* is a manifesto. It comes at a propitious time; the online world has been hyped beyond recognition. ... Few people have more impressive credentials to trash the Internet than Stoll.

Hmm, try telling that to the poor sod who was just about to set up an online auction site, but then decided against it after reading Stoll's book. Or the equally sad character who was offered the chance to invest in an online bookstore named after a rainforest, but declined for the same reason. You get the picture.

As for Stoll today? Well, he's still an astronomer, but he's also dabbled in sales. He sells something called Klein Bottles. Online. Irony can be such a cruel e-mistress.

1995 was also the year that net legend and inventor of the Ethernet, Robert Metcalfe saw fit to tell the readers of his *InfoWorld* column that the internet would,

> ... go spectacularly supernova and in 1996 catastrophically collapse.

By August 1996 it hadn't gone supernova, in fact it hadn't even gone nova, but there were a couple of fairly big glitches at Netcom and America Online which only served to confirm Bob's suspicions. '*This is only the beginning*', he said before going on to predict a gigalapse, which is apparently an internet blackout of a billion 'person hours'.

Bob was wrong, spectacularly, supernovaly and catastrophically, but, admirably, having originally said that he would eat his words if he was proved to be incorrect, in 1997 at the Sixth WWW International Conference he put a hard copy of his original 1995 column into a food blender along with some liquid, switched it on and then proceeded to down the lot. Nuff respec'.

A couple of years later the internet continued to function gigatastically well, though Bob remained stuck in the khazi painfully passing the last of his column, so it was time for him to hand the mantle of being w.w.w. (wrong. wrong. wrong) over to David Komansky, at the time CEO of Merrill Lynch, the investment bank soon to bring the financial world to its knees. No doubt David's clients and investors would have been overjoyed with this little utterance of his.

There will never be a market in selling stock over the internet.

Finally and fittingly we come to Mr Bill Gates, a man who has done so ludicrously well, you'd think it'd be wise to hang off his every word. There's the exception to every rule though, as these eight he chose to utter in 2004 prove:

Two years from now, spam will be solved.

If anyone was going to sort it out it was him and given that he hasn't already done so, it seems spam will continue to plague us for the foreseeable future (damn – we just made a prediction – retract, retract – shit, it's too late).

SPACE

With countless other galaxies zillions of miles beyond our own, humans can be forgiven for sometimes feeling rather small and insignificant. It's not a pleasant feeling, but perhaps this is why, when it comes to space, some people have tried to make themselves big and significant, by making glittering prophecies about all that is 'out there'.

Since our earliest presence on Earth (not the amoeba stage, a bit later) we've been looking into the night sky and asking questions such as; 'Is that speeding bolt of white light going to kill us,' and 'Why does that cluster of stars look like a penguin's backside?' Those who were really interested started making elementary 'viewing screens' to see things better; in fact the macho-science battle to make the world's longest/largest/most powerful telescope continues today.

As with all subjects of human fascination there were plenty of folk more than willing to make predictions about the stars, the planets and whatever else they thought they saw out in the vastness up above. As ever, some predictors got carried away and proclaimed that alien-human dance troupes would soon be formed, doing intergalactic tours and making their strange warbly show tunes freely accessible as universe-wide downloads. Some, on the other hand, were negative and sceptical, refuting any talk of future space travel and showdowns with aliens despite the fact that we all know every American president since Abraham Lincoln has been a Jupitan Overlord in human form.

1. Put your toy rockets back in your pram and grow up

At one time most people thought that the earth was both flat and at the centre of the Universe, so it's little wonder then that history is littered with those who poured scorn on anyone who dared suggest things might be different up in the heavens and its surrounds.

Martin Luther was one such cynic. In the 16th century he called Copernicus (the father of modern astronomy) a fool for daring to suggest such nonsense as the earth rotated on its own axis.

Then there was Father Augustin de Angelis, who, in response to a new theory about comets that Isaac Newton was working on said in 1673 that, *'comets are not heavenly bodies, but originate in the earth's atmosphere below the moon'.*

While Martin and Augustin were both astronomically wrong, it's kind of understandable for them to have been so given the time periods they lived in and the state of scientific knowledge at their disposal.

Cut to the 20th century and it's somewhat less easy to be so forgiving about those who poo poo'd anything that challenged the accepted order of things. Take A.W. Bickerton, for example, a New Zealand scientist and damned clever chap. He used specific mathematical calculations to predict that space hopping would never happen. Here he is in 1926:

This foolish idea of shooting at the moon is an example of the absurd length to which vicious specialisation will carry scientists working in thought-tight compartments. ... For a projectile entirely to escape the gravitation of the earth, it needs a velocity of 7 miles a second. The thermal energy of a gramme at this speed is 15180 calories. ... The energy of our most violent explosive – nitroglycerin – is less than 1500 calories per gramme. Consequently, even had the explosive nothing to carry, it has only one tenth of the energy to escape the earth ... hence the proposition appears to be basically unsound.

Of a similar mind to Bickerton was American uber-inventor Lee De Forest. With patents aplenty to his name you'd imagine he'd be open to all sorts of new and radical ideas, looking to get in on the action and patent yet more gadgets that might be useful to astronauts of the future. Well, if his 1926 prediction about space travel is anything to go by this was one particular business opportunity he wasn't going to get a piece of.

To place a man in a multi-stage rocket and project him into the controlling gravitational field of the moon where the passengers can make scientific observations, perhaps land alive, and then return to Earth – all that constitutes a wild dream worthy of Jules Verne. I am bold enough to say that such a man-made voyage will never occur regardless of all future advances.

The absurdity of claiming that it is bold to discount every single innovation there will ever be is palpable for all to see.

Having built the bandwagon, Bickerton and De Forest set it off on its travels for others to jump on. First to do so was professor of Astronomy at the University of Chicago, Dr F.R. Moulton – curiously the 'F' is for Forest. In 1932 he was all for keeping his feet firmly on the ground when talking about space travel.

There is no hope for the fanciful idea of reaching the moon, because of insurmountable barriers to escaping the earth's gravity.

Strange how those insurmountable barriers didn't prevent the good doctor from having a crater on the moon named after him.

So far the idea of landing on the moon has been called foolish, a wild dream and fanciful; perhaps the *New York Times* of 1936 will add another ever so slightly haughty adjective to that list.

A rocket will never be able to leave the earth's atmosphere.

Oh well, what the prediction lacked in both accuracy and description was more than made up for in succinctness.

As the world entered the 1950s those making outlandishly negative pronouncements on the possibility of space travel had even fewer excuses, especially given that Germany had launched the first rocket that could fly high enough to get into space in 1942 and America had done likewise in 1946, only theirs obviously wasn't the first.

Yes, the space race was well and truly off and running, but that didn't deter the optimistically challenged such as Astronomer Royal and space advisor to the British government Dr Richard van der Riet Woolley. But then, he already had form on the negative side of the fence.

The whole procedure [of shooting rockets into space] ... presents difficulties of so fundamental a nature, that we are forced to dismiss the notion as essentially impracticable.

That was in 1936 and clearly the advances made over the next 20 years did precisely nothing to make him change his mind because, in 1956, he told *Time* magazine that he still believed all talk of space travel was way off the mark:

It's utter bilge. I don't think anybody will ever put up enough money to do such a thing. ... What good would it do us? If we spent the same amount of money on preparing first-class

astronomical equipment we would learn much more about the
universe. ... It is all rather rot.

The following year, *Sputnik* orbited the earth.

To have one Astronomer Royal lay into the possibility of
space flight is unfortunate; to have two is downright care-
lessness. But incredibly, that's exactly what happened. Woolley
took over the post from Sir Harold Spencer Jones, and what did
Jones do after his successor made the above declaration? He
waited until *two weeks* before *Sputnik* orbited the earth to say:

Space travel is bunk.

It was clear that in 1950s Britain you just couldn't get Astronomer Royals, but, rather than being dragged out of his ivory
tower, clamped into the stocks and publicly derided, Spencer
Jones also had a crater on the moon named after him. And one
on Mars. Oh, and an asteroid.

People didn't just knock the idea of putting a man into
space though, they also down talked any related advancements.
T.A.M. Craven – his name was Tunis Augustus McDonough,
which might explain why he preferred to be known by his
initials – was an American naval officer with a specialism in
communications. He was pretty good at his job, so much so
that President Franklin D. Roosevelt, no less, promoted him to
Chief Engineer to the Federal Communications Commission,
which could explain why, in 1961, he felt he had the authority
to audaciously declare:

There is practically no chance communications space satellites
will be used to provide better telephone, telegraph, television, or
radio service inside the United States.

What d'ya know? The first commercial communications sat-
ellite was hoisted into service in 1965, something that Craven

himself must have rued somewhat, not least because it meant that his prediction could now reach a far wider audience.

2. Slow down, the moon isn't going anywhere

Within the solar system of space predictions there's a small, but delightful sub-category of people who believed that space travel and a moon landing would definitely happen, but who, when it came to estimating *when* it would happen, erred on the side of caution and missed out on the actual date, sometimes by a considerable batch of years.

At the forefront of this slow-date-setting movement were the good folk at *Look* magazine who, in December 1957, two months after that launch of *Sputnik 1*, set out a time line for future space related achievements.

> Piloted satellite will mark man's first venture into outer space. . . . It will come only after long experience with unmanned satellites. Best-informed opinion places the date with the decade 1970 to 1980.

Interesting to speculate as to exactly what they meant by '*best-informed opinion*'. It's possible that they had a hot line to NASA, but it's equally likely that they were referring to the magazine's Science editor and the wild imaginings of his or her mind with a deadline fast approaching.

From the Seventies they, quite understandably and logically, considered the Eighties.

> A trip around the moon in a rocket ship launched either from a space platform or from the earth's surface (depending on tech-nological developments) will be the next step. . . . Experts believe that will come in the decade 1980–1990.

Yes, of course, the Eighties, the decade of new romantics, big hair and trips round the moon. Up next, in case you haven't worked it out, the Nineties.

> A landing on the moon ... man's goal for as long as he has had the imagination to think about it, will be made in the last decade of this century.

Well there's a thing. *'Man's goal for as long as he has had the imagination to think about it'*. It's a curious turn of phrase and no mistake; it's as if they're saying the moment someone looked up at the moon and thought, 'Ooh, I'd like to go there', marked the dawn of human imagination. From that point on we were able to imagine and think creatively. Or, conversely, perhaps, the second after we'd evolved an imagination, the very first imaginative thought was about going to the moon.

The possibilities are, well, twofold, but given that all of the magazine's predictions had in fact happened by July 1969, the chances are they had let their imaginations run away with them.

A few years later *New Scientist* magazine got in on the temporally incorrect act. In 1964, having watched developments with a very close, not to mention scientific eye, they felt sure that President Kennedy's pronouncements on the American space programme were overly optimistic and ran the risk of letting all of his citizens down, not to mention giving the Ruskies top spot on the space-race podium:

> The odds are now that the United States will not be able to honour the 1970 manned-lunar-landing date set by Mr Kennedy.

In 1969 Neil Armstrong and Buzz Aldrin hit Mr Kennedy's target and trumped the Russians.

3. A world of endless possibilities part 1 – pre-moon landing

In the late 1950s many people, especially some leading scientists and astronomers, were starting to get very worked up about space travel. The moon, which had seemed so distant and un-landable-on to their ancestors, was suddenly within reach. It was possible, even probable, that before too long a human being would set foot on its surface. Dash it; an earth-moon space train could soon be in action complete with zero-gravity buffet cars.

Okay, so in actual fact most people remained fairly level-headed and frankly, quite dull, about the prospect, but thankfully others were so excited by the whole scenario that they began to make predictions way over and above a simple moon landing. One of these leftfield-thinking types was the United States postmaster general in the late Fifties, Arthur Summerfield.

The cause of Summerfield's over-excitement was an experiment his US Postal Service carried out in June 1959. A naval ship, the SS *Barbero*, stationed off the northern Florida coast, fired a Regulus cruise missile towards the Naval Auxiliary Air Station, in Mayport, Florida. As these things go, blowing Mayport to kingdom come in the name of scientific inquiry might seem a little overly 'experimental', but all was not as it seemed. After a 22-minute flight this particular missile landed smoothly in Mayport. It didn't explode because its nuclear warhead had been replaced by two Post Office Department Mail Containers with a combined payload of 3,000 letters. (Thank God whoever was responsible for doing that was on the ball.)

It was an experiment looking into the delivery of mail by missile and Summerfield was so enthused by its apparent success that he was moved to make quite a rash pronouncement on the subject.

Before man reaches the moon, mail will be delivered within hours

from New York to California, to Britain, to India or Australia by
guided missiles. We stand on the threshold of rocket mail.

We didn't stand on it, or anywhere near it for that matter,
because rocket mail isn't really cost effective. Cruise missiles
don't come cheap, unless you know the right people in Iran,
and replacing those nuclear warheads is not really a job for a
postal worker no matter how highly trained they might be.
Mind you, if Summerfield's prediction had been correct, how
the devil would countries be able to tell the difference between
cruise missiles carrying thermo-nuclear bombs and those carrying Christmas cards? Maybe they could be painted in different
colours or have special markings; a skull and cross bones for a
weapon of mass destruction and a jolly glowing Santa for a
yuletide greeting?

Fast forward three years and levels of expectation were
increasing still further. Even though no earthling had set foot
on the moon's delightfully cratery surface, people were imagin-
ing all sorts of radical travel developments, and when it came
to outer space predictions the organisers of the 1962 Seattle
World Fair certainly weren't going to miss out.

Supersonic air travel will allow people to circumnavigate the world
in minutes.

Just think about that. In the time it takes to make a vegetarian
moussaka, you could have been to Australia and back, twice.
Actually, if there was an ingredient you wanted to put into your
moussaka that was only available in Australia, you could pop
there, get it and return in time for your dinner party. Only you
couldn't. Even if it was possible to travel around the globe
in minutes, you'd still have to check in two hours before
take off and then spend another couple of hours getting
through customs at your destination, followed by six hours
trying to locate your luggage, which would probably have

circumnavigated the globe 14 more times before being returned to you. Might be best just to nip to the local corner shop to get that missing ingredient.

A couple of years later and those studying the future decided it was time to get a little more scientific, so they developed something called The Delphi Technique. In essence this brilliant breakthrough involved asking a number of experts to make predictions in private, i.e. without knowing what the others were saying, and then collating the results together in a forecast. It's marvellous, not least because it provides an opportunity for loads of people to be wrong, rather than just one, which is precisely what happened when the technique was used in a September 1964 long-range forecasting study by T.J. Gordon and Olaf Helmer.

It's a massive document, but in the section 'Predicted Progress in Space', we're told to expect a manned Mars and Venus fly-by towards the end of the Seventies, a permanent moon base in the early Eighties and a manned landing on Mars most likely by the mid Eighties. They were ambitious and we like that. They were wrong and we like that too.

Another year on and things were getting proper mental. A 1965 edition of the *Chicago Tribune* quoted a local real estate broker by the name of Walter P. Kuehnle, who had popped over to the congress of the 19-nation International Real Estate federation in Belgium and informed the assembled throng that,

> By the year 2000, business conventions will be held at interplanetary 'cosmotels,' to which most delegates will travel in their own family 'volkscapsules' or 'satellacs.'

Considering that there can be nothing more mind numbingly tedious than a gathering of the 19-nation International Real Estate federation, you could be forgiven for thinking that Walter made this prediction to liven proceedings up a little, but there is no record of him delivering this part of his address with a smile on his face or even a hint of irony, so one must assume that not to be the case.

Given that, his vision is banal in the extreme. Not a five star luxury hotel in the plushest part of Venus for the estate agent of the future, no. A bleeding cosmotel on the outskirts of the Ishtar Terra. That's going to go down well isn't it?

Then there are the brilliantly named vehicles that the future delegates are going to be travelling in. It's just about possible to imagine a 'volkscapsule', a Volkswagen with rocket boosters perhaps, but what on earth he envisioned a 'satellac' to be is anyone's guess.

Even worse though is Walter's use of the word 'family' to precede these new forms of transport. It implies that in the year 2000 balding businessmen in their mid-fifties, wouldn't be driving around in really cool, convertible volkscapsules or satellacs that go from nought to the speed of light in 3.6 seconds and just might see them cop a feel with a young secretary. Rather they'd be pootling about space in a hatchback family satellac with kiddie seats in the back, and a 'Little Princess On Board' sign attached to the rear window.

As estate agents everywhere despaired at the thought of what the future held in store for them, everyone else rejoiced in the fact that the oily, male, middle-aged percentage-grabbing bastards among them were finally going to get what they deserved – a dullard's family car. If only it had come true.

4. A world of endless possibilities part 2 – post-moon landing

On 21 July 1969 Neil Armstrong stepped out of the craft, descended the ladder and placed his left foot on the moon's surface. While some may have predicted this moment, what no one could have foreseen was that he was going to fluff his lines.

That's one small step for [a] man, one giant leap for mankind.

The parentheses around the 'a' are due to the fact that Armstrong insisted he did say the 'a', but millions watching on TV or listening on radios didn't hear it.

Actually what he said about the incident was that he *'would hope that history would grant me leeway for dropping the syllable and understand that it was certainly intended, even if it was not said – although it might actually have been,'* which certainly cleared things up.

Either way it was a pretty epic moment in the relatively short lifespan of the human race. It also had the galvanising effect of making some people go absolutely nuts with their space-related predictions such as Gerald Snyder for one.

Snyder wrote the 1973 book, *1994 – The World of Tomorrow*, a tome which contains within its pages several startling forecasts. Indeed, with the moon landing already four long years in the past, you can almost hear Gerald saying: 'Moon? Pa! That is so yesteryear!' as he tells us that,

Toward the end of the twentieth century, manned trips to Venus also can be expected.

The moon is approximately a quarter of a million miles from earth and getting people up there was a pretty big deal. Venus is about 25 million miles away, that's an awfully long time to spend in space singing, ''twas on the good ship Venus', to say nothing of the fact that surface temperatures on the planet can exceed 460 degrees Celsius. That could lead to quite a different first line from the astronaut.

That's one small step for man, one ... Jesus, it's hot ... arrrggghhh, my foot's on fire ... [arrrrgggghhhhh] ...

The second arrrrgggghhhhh is in parentheses because there is some debate as to whether the astronaut would get a chance to utter it or would have been burnt to a cinder by that point.

Undeterred though, Snyder continues envisioning yet more space conquests.

... in the early twenty-first century, manned spacecraft may be approaching the ringed planet of Saturn.

Here's the maths; a return trip to Saturn is in the region of a billion and a half miles. Spaceships would have to up their speeds phenomenally to make it there and back in time for, well, anything really, unless people lived well into their 200s, but even then, you'd probably run out of conversation with your fellow crew members after the first hundred million miles, spend the next hundred millions miles in complete silence before going completely insane and killing everyone else on board by the time you'd passed the three hundred million mile mark, by which point you wouldn't even be halfway there.

But this wasn't the end of Snyder's soothsaying.

One forecast for the year 2002 predicts two thousand people living on the moon and ten people on Mars.

Ten people living on Mars? Why not 9 or 11? It's not a bus or a plane – 'sorry sir, we're full, you'll have to get the next one' – it's a planet for God's sake, and a bloody massive one at that.

Snyder didn't just envisage colonies on the moon and Mars though; he saw a whole host of tantalising possibilities – things that would not be available to mere mortals living within the earth's atmosphere. Like Arthur Radebaugh before him (see Health and the Human Body, pp. 72–3) Snyder predicted that medical science could best progress by launching itself into the rarefied air of space:

In the gravity-free wards of space hospitals ... patients with heart
ailments might be treated in ways that would help them live
longer. The germ-free and zero-gravity environment of space
might also offer special comfort to people suffering from severe
burns and other ailments.

But these treatments wouldn't be solely for those who were
already ill. A 'physiologist' quoted in the book says:

I can envision executives and other people leaving their terrestrial
jobs for their annual physicals and rest in space. Preventative
maintenance would be performed on them in the orbital health
maintenance station.

It's heartening to know that when set aside from 'executives'
the rest of us are merely 'other people'. Why can't we be referred
to as 'non-executives' or 'people who don't earn very much
money?'

The crucial question though is, would these annual check-
ups be available on the NHS? The answer, one feels, is highly
predictable and thus perhaps 'other people' should be removed
from the equation altogether.

1994 – The World of Tomorrow's ten people living on Mars is
minuscule when compared to the figure envisaged by L. Eugene
Root – a man who at one time had been president of Lockheed
Missiles and Space Company, and president of the American
Aeronautical Sciences. He believed that in the late 1980s the
United States would send the first manned expedition to Mars,
and that this would be followed by a series of other expeditions.
With so many people and so much equipment being trans-
ported to Mars, Root believed the next logical step would be to
create a permanent community up there:

The city has an average population of over four thousand people,
although even the permanent residents are assumed to return to

Earth every six months. The stay time of the residents ranges
from a minimum of three weeks to six months for technicians,
workers and staff support personnel.

Let's take a closer look at those figures for an earth second.
Residents' 'stay time' would start with a minimum of three
weeks. THREE WEEKS. What kind of space dust was Root
snacking on when he made this pronouncement? You travel
millions and millions of miles to get to Mars and then limit
your stay to just three weeks? That's the equivalent of popping
to Tasmania and then returning home a few minutes later. It's
the red planet for goodness' sake; no one in their right mind is
going to make the 47 million mile trip back to Earth just
because they've run out of toothpaste.

1982 saw the publication of the *Omni Future Almanac*, a space
agey, futuristicy classic within whose pages are some predictive
wonders, such as this curious morsel.

By 2000, more than 1,000 people live and work on the moon,
a slight majority of them female, according to NASA predictions.

NASA there, still clinging to the women-do-housework theory
and planning carefully for all the cooking and cleaning needed
on the moon base.

More wondrous though was a prediction that had astro-
nautical bodyguards everywhere jumping for joy at their future
employment prospects.

Enough people will be present in space by 2000 to make 'space
crime' an issue.

Space muggings, rocketjacking and drifting grifters, it's enough
to make lexicographers specialising in crime words pull their
hair out.

As to whose jurisdiction some of these crimes might come under, well, it's a tricky one. Under Martian law if a pet cat floats into a neighbour's garden, it's not illegal for the neighbour to claim ownership of the cat, whereas on Uranus, the cat has to remain within the orbit of the neighbour's garden of its own free will for over six hours – the free will element was introduced after one neighbour tied a floating cat to his shed for six hours to prevent it floating back into its owner's garden.

5. Frankly, it's an intergalactic CSI minefield

We're all going on a summer holiday, no more working for a light year or two.

Everyone looks forward to future exotic holidays, no one more so than Neil Ardley, author of the book *School, Work and Play (World of Tomorrow)*. It was published in 1981, though incredibly the above-mentioned 1973 book, *1994 – The World of Tomorrow*, didn't contain a prediction that someone else would nick its title.

That aside, within the pages of this volume, Ardley looked ahead to *where* we would soon all be vacationing and also how we would go about making the necessary arrangements. To this end he predicted that human beings would be able to avoid all the unpleasant jobs associated with booking a holiday, as these would be completed by super-intelligent computers or as he called them 'Home Videophone Computers'. Instead of tearing out great clumps of hair while sitting in a travel agency listening to a ring tone seven thousand times before someone finally says: 'Hi, this is Angela from Thomas Cook I need two seats to Miami leaving next Thursday at 8:40, one lacto-vegetarian meal, please' or cursing your laptop (having spent five hours on it) for crashing a second before that great value break was booked, these new super-intelligent computers would book a break at a destination you'll be guaranteed to love, in a price range that perfectly suits your wallet, while also arranging your travel insurance, transport for every stage of the journey, suitable day trips, currency needs and, if required, the pro-curement of a mid-length grass skirt – all within a matter of seconds.

To be fair, Ardley was on the right lines when it came to computers, but he failed to factor in human idiocy, and thus while modern computers might be intelligent, the people oper-ating them most definitely aren't; if anything, booking a holiday now is more stressful and time-consuming than at any time in human history.

He also failed to mention what use the super-computers would be if your flight was delayed or cancelled, or if the villa that looked so good in the brochure was actually a disused tuna storage facility, with the accompanying pungent aroma.

While the first part of his vision just about fell within the realms of possibility, when it came to the second part Ardley became a standard-bearer for the off-beam 'Holidays in Space' brigade, envisaging the creation of the 'Space Islands' – a holiday paradise consisting of:

> A group of huge space colonies that are resorts for people from Earth, the Moonbase and other space colonies. These colonies will have different climates in order to attract all kinds of tourists, and you choose a colony that is like several South Sea islands inside. However, unlike the real South Sea islands, you can play weightless games there and experience other such delights that only the Space Islands can offer.

One can only imagine what these 'other such delights' are, but presumably, in Ardley's holiday universe, the hotels would be lavish, the gravity boots would be haute couture and the meals magnificent, all prepared by a phalanx of kitchen robots schooled by a metallic Gordon Ramsay look-alike. What's more, due to the weightless atmosphere, you could stuff yourself silly with Jupiterian doughnuts and not put on an ounce. However, if you were feeling guilty about how much you're eating, you could always burn off a few calories in those 'Weightless games,' although Frisbee throwing could be extremely lengthy, as you'd have to wait for your disc to circumnavigate Pluto before returning.

Of course, once you've been in your space resort for a few days, you're going to want to explore a little; well fear not, according to Ardley, the possibilities for doing so are manifold.

> Then it's off on a whole variety of robot transports as exciting as the vacation itself – beltways, autotaxis, high-speed monorail trains, underground vacuum bullet trains, mammoth jets, space shuttles and finally a spacecruiser out of the colony.

To be honest, if a trip on a beltway is as exciting as the vacation itself, it might have been better to stay on Earth.

Having started with computers Ardley brings them back in a delightful closing of the circle by predicting the following:

> You're there at last, and a wonderful vacation lies before you. There's only one problem – no one speaks English. The Space Islands are designed to suit all the people on Earth, and so their languages vary. You've chosen one in which Spanish is spoken. You can't speak Spanish, so you hire a portable computer that translates instantly from one language to another.

Thank goodness for those translating computers, because if they didn't exist you might have to learn to speak a bit of Spanish, and that's just too far-fetched for anyone's imagination.

All told Ardley paints a wonderful picture of the holiday of tomorrow, but one thing will never change; come what may, no matter how early you get up, you still won't be able to get to the hover sunbeds first; the Space Germans will already be there.

A year after Ardley's meisterwerk another seminal book was published. *The Kids' Whole Future Catalogue – A Book about Your Future!* by Paula Taylor looked 20 years into the future and shouted loudly from the cover that it was: *'Full of facts and photos – plus lots of things to send for!'* There were indeed many things to send for, but as for being full of facts, well, we'll let you be the judge of that.

In a section entitled 'Vacation at a Space Hotel', we're introduced to 'Jenny' who is staying at a space hotel and has written a letter to her friend Susan telling her all about it. (Surely by then they would have had letter-writing computers to do that sort of thing.)

> Dear Susan,
>
> We arrived at the space hotel yesterday, and the first thing I did was try out the swimming pool. It really is as much fun

as everyone says, but the low gravity takes getting used to. Everything happens more slowly than usual – you feel as though you're part of a movie that's being shown in slow motion. When you jump off the diving board, you can easily do two or three somersaults before you hit the water – and when you do go in, you leave a hole, which takes a few seconds to fill up. The pool doesn't look anything like the ones on Earth. It's like an enormous barrel with water lining the inside. The barrel rotates very slowly, creating just enough force to keep the water pushed up against the sides. When you're in the pool, you can see water curving uphill and people swimming upside down overhead. As if that isn't strange enough, you can also see people floating through the air in the zero-g area at the center of the barrel. To get there, all you have to do is jump high off the diving board and flap your arms like wings. If you hold a paddle in each hand, it's easier to steer. I want to tell you about all the other things I've done, but there isn't time. I'll write again tomorrow.

Love, Jenny

Of course, if Jenny's space hotel happened to be on Venus, where one day is equivalent to 243 Earth days, Susan would be waiting quite a while for that next letter. Also, while the swimming pool does sound like a lot of fun, by using the abbreviation 'zero-g', Jenny has unfortunately marked herself out as a bit of a twat and thus it's no wonder she's gone away on her own.

It's possible that Jenny was not on holiday, but on a business trip, buying supplies for her family's shop back on Earth because another prediction in *The Kids' Whole Future Catalogue* told us that,

In the future, products from space will be in great demand. Economists are predicting a 20 billion dollar market for space-made goods by the year 2000.

One can only hope that the selfsame economists made huge investments of their own money based on their prediction.

6. Extra stupid terrestrials

For thousands of years humans have hoped for a clear night so that they can look up at the stars and wonder if anyone else is out there. Sky-gazer after sky-gazer has attempted to make contact with our potential planetary neighbours in the vain hope that they will be able to go on breakfast TV and declare they're the first person to enjoy human-alien contact. But is this wise? Not according to genius physicist Stephen Hawking.

Hawking knows what he's talking about when it comes to space-related matters and his line on trying to contact aliens is DON'T DO IT; or in his words, 'lay low'. In *A Brief History of Time*, Hawking suggests that 'alerting' potential extraterrestrial intelligences to our existence is a reckless thing to do for the simple reason that if they have bigger and better guns than us, they'll blow us all to kingdom come. He based this observation not on the *Men in Black* trilogy, but on the way human civilisations have historically acted when they've come across other human civilisations less well equipped than themselves. But do people listen to him? Do they buggery.

Back in the 19th century scientists and astronomers were so keen to actually attract aliens that they laid down plans to create gigantic canals of flame in the Sahara desert and enormous earthworks in Siberia. Of the two, the former is certainly a dubious way of enticing a passing group of ETs to land. Surely they'd just think, 'oh my God, the place is on fire, let's go to Mars instead.'

Another who reckoned that it would all be lovely and cordial with our alien chums was American political activist, Mary E. Lease who in 1893 predicted that at some point in the next hundred years,

We will hold communication with the inhabitants of other planets, and Sunday excursions to the mountains of the moon will not excite comment.

If Stephen Hawking's warning turned out to be correct and the aliens did have more sophisticated weapons than humans, before Mary could take one step of a Sunday excursion, she'd be blown to smithereens by the aliens' powerful ray guns.

By 1900, quite possibly because those canal flames were never lit, aliens had still not shown up, but when asked to look ahead into the new millennium, scientists were convinced that at some point in the ensuing years we'd talk with Martians who, for reasons that remain inexplicable, might resemble giant dragonflies with wingspans of 72 feet.

Come 1947 and no alien life force, dragonfly-like or otherwise, had shown up, but then came the infamous 'Roswell incident', whereby debris of some sort of 'craft' was found near Roswell, New Mexico, which had many postulating that aliens had dropped in for a visit and the government were covering it up. Remarkably though, after the initial brouhaha, UFO watchers generally let the issue lie and though the Fifties and Sixties saw lots of other reported 'sightings' and alien predictions, it wasn't until the 1970s that the floodgates really opened.

In 1973 a man named Stephen Pulaski claimed that he'd entered a UFO and held face-to-face talks with a group of aliens. Hanging out on their craft was also, apparently, the Grim Reaper himself. Chewing the fat, Grimmy told Pulaski that the world would be vanquished in 1976. Pulaski thought it only fair that he share his encounter with the rest of humanity, though, when 1976 passed without earthly destruction, but a very hot summer instead, for some reason he wasn't able to return to the UFO to ask what had gone wrong.

Then in 1978 the name 'Roswell' reared its head again – big time. Major Jesse Marcel, who was involved with the original recovery of the debris in 1947, was interviewed by ufologist Stanton T. Friedman. In this interview, Marcel revealed that he thought Roswell *had* been a government cover up and that it *was* an alien craft that had landed. Next thing you know half of the United States are claiming to have seen a UFO, met an extra-terrestrial or had an alien probe inserted into their rectum, and of course, predicting all manner of things based on information gleaned from their new alien best friends. And, as the 20th century dissolved into the 21st century, in spite of the fact that no one had gathered one scintilla of evidence that aliens did exist, the forecasts kept coming.

At the start of the new millennium, Charles Spiegel, a retired psychology professor predicted that the ancient city of Atlantis would emerge from the Caribbean sometime in 2001. What's that got to do with aliens you might reasonably ask? Well, Spiegel went on to claim that, once risen, a thousand ETs in 33 spaceships would set out from 'Myton' and land in Atlantis whereupon they'd bestow on humankind some revealing titbits of knowledge and wisdom. You could perhaps say that what he predicted was 2001: A Space Oddity.

Elsewhere, cult leader Yaweh (real name Ramon Watkins) predicted that when he arranged a 'prayer caravan' on a 'holy mountain' outside of LA, alien spaceships would travel down to meet him. In fact, he claims to have the ability to summon UFOs on demand, but despite posting many videos of such events online, in none of them do the summoned crafts come close enough to the camera to provide unequivocal evidence of his abilities. Just his rotten luck that the only aliens he is able to summon turn out to be camera shy.

Another who foresaw the early part of the 21st century as the time that terrestrials of the extra variety would be putting 'Earth' into their sat navs was Indian astrologer, Bejan Daruwalla.

On our Republic Day 2008, we will be visited by aliens. The best part of it is, we will know it and accept it.

Doesn't sound all that great does it? Why couldn't the best part of it be that they'd teach us how to become immortal and regain our youth?

Australia's Blossom Goodchild isn't an astrologer, preferring instead to call herself a 'Chaneller.' However, like Daruwalla, she noted 2008 as alien year. Blossom claimed to have made contact with an alien force that would be appearing in a huge spaceship over the 'American Desert' that year, but rather than come here intent on destruction as Stevie Hawking would have it, according to Blossom these aliens would;

> Come in love to help us and our planet move to a new higher vibration of love.

Interestingly, had Blossom been right it would have meant those poor aliens schlepping from India to Australia and then more than likely, on elsewhere. In fact, in order to recoup a little of the expense it cost them to travel here they could undertake a world tour earning extra income by selling 'Aliens World Tour 2008' t-shirts.

Another of a similar ilk is psychic David Wilcock who in July 2009 predicted that before the end of the year, the United States government would stage a two-hour international event during which they would finally tell the truth about the alien presence on planet Earth. He knew about this because a source had told him and he also knew that the two-hour TV spot had already been booked. Well, if it had it did disastrously in the ratings with viewing figures of approximately zero.

But while all of the previous forecasters ended up looking like charlatans when their prophecies didn't take place, one man came up with his own ingenious prediction method that he believed was foolproof: Say you already *know* what the future holds because you *come from the future.*

The name John Titor started appearing on various internet sites at the start of the Noughties. Titor claimed he was a time traveller from 2036 whose original mission had been to go back to 1975 to get his hands on an IBM 5100. Returning to his own time he would use the IBM computer to 'debug' various infected computer programmes that were in use in 2036. Coming, as he did, from 2036, Titor could, quite understandably tell people what was going to unfold in their future, so when he told everyone that another civil war would break out in America in 2004 there really was no reason not to believe him; until 2004 came and went and no civil war took place.

When it came to aliens Titor hedged his bets ever so slightly by saying that in 2036 UFOs were still things of great mystery to humans, but that they might be peopled by beings much further into the future than 2036, who possessed better time machines than the one he travelled in. Well then why didn't he ... oh forget it.

7. *Edward Mukaka Nkoloso's Guide To The Galaxy*

The last word on this matter goes to that giant of space exploration, Edward Mukaka Nkoloso. Edward was a science teacher from Zambia who, in the early Sixties, set up the Zambia National Academy of Science, Space Research and Philosophy. The aim was to send twelve astronauts and ten cats in a rocket to Mars and Nkoloso was confident.

I'll have my first Zambian astronaut on the moon by 1965 ... using my own firing system derived from the catapult. ... I'm getting my astronauts acclimatized to space travel by placing them in my space capsule every day. It's a 40 gallon oil drum in which they sit, and I then roll them down a hill. This gives them the feeling of rushing through space. I also make them swing from the end of a long rope. When they reach the highest point, I cut the rope. This produces the feeling of free fall.

To fund his ambitious project Eddie asked the UN for about

$20 million, but when this wasn't forthcoming he approached the Americans and suggested the two countries work together, on one condition. *'When the two astronauts step on to the moon, the Zambian flag goes up first.'* Amazingly, the Americans declined this kind offer and decided to go it alone.

As for Eddie's endeavour, unfortunately his main female astronaut fell pregnant and was removed from the project by her parents, a blow from which the Zambia National Academy of Science, Space Research and Philosophy never really recovered.

THE END OF THE WORLD

If there's one prediction that can lay claim to being the daddy of them all, it's that old apocalyptic chestnut; the end of the world. Chances are the very first such prediction was made somewhere between one yoctosecond (a quadrillionth of a second) and one zeptosecond (a sextillionth of a second) after the Big Bang, when a rapidly expanding and cooling particle of something or other turned to a rapidly expanding and cooling particle of something else and shrugged, 'I give it about another attosecond (a quintillionth of a second)'.

Of course that's just a complete guess, but then so, it seems, is just about every prophecy that predicted the world would have ended by now, all of which have one thing in common; they were wrong, every single last one of them. At the time of writing this book, the world is most definitely still here, though it may not be by the time it's out in the shops, because American religious broadcaster, Harold Camping, has predicted that life as we know it will end on 21 October 2011 – co-incidentally the exact date of publication (fancy that). So, if you're reading fragments of this text on a charred piece of paper in an unknown universe, with angels or devilish creatures leaning over your shoulder, Camping was probably right. If however, you're holding it in its pristine form and planet Earth is still around, Camping got it wrong.

Incredibly though, the fact that all the previous predictions have ranged from wildly inaccurate to ludicrously erroneous hasn't deterred great swathes of people from putting their necks, and their self-respect, on the line, and boldly stating the exact moment of our little planet's demise.

Frankly, in the world of predictions, it's a schoolboy/girl error, and not only because if it turns out to be wrong you'll never be able to show your face in polite society again. Worse still, if it turns out to be right, you won't be around to bask in the glory. In fact, you won't even have time to say, 'I warned you!' before we're all on our way to kingdom come. At least if you make a prediction about hotels on Venus by the year 2050 which somehow turns out to be correct, you can then humbly receive the plaudits that your incredible soothsaying ability deserves (as long as no one mentions your other prediction about intelligent robot ants acting as hotel car parking valets).

The other error that abounds is to tell everyone that the end of the world is coming, or the end of the world is upon us. It's not. Everyone knows that if you're going to predict Arma-geddon, there's a quasi-legal requirement to use the word nigh; which is good, as the poor word doesn't get out much does it? People don't say, 'it's nighly quarter to eight' and kids don't moan, 'are we nighly there yet?' So the very least you can do as a bona fide end of the world predictor, is to give the word 'nigh' its due, and use it when you make your calamitous prediction.

All told, no one's come close to predicting the end of the world correctly, clearly it's nigh on impossible (hang on a minute . . .), but one thing that can be said with deadly accuracy is that until Earth does explode, implode or simply vanish, there'll be no end to the end of the world predictions.

Top marks for the sign. Zero marks for the prediction.

1. The world will end in 2,800 BC

Technically this is inaccurate not only because 2,800 BC has come and gone, but also because it's not actually a predicted date for the end of the world. Rather it is the date those carbon dating wizards have assigned to an Assyrian clay tablet upon which the following is written:

> Our earth is degenerate in these latter days. There are signs that the world is speedily coming to an end. Bribery and corruption are common.

The ambiguity is over 'speedily', which, given the pace of life in old Assyria could mean anything from a couple of weeks to ten years; nonetheless it is the first recorded end of the world prediction, though not, as whoever wrote it presumably imagined, the last.

It could of course have been written by someone who was

simply having a bad day and further excavations might yet find another tablet bearing the words, 'Sorry, was just a bit pissed off about King Shamshi-Adad's new tax on oxen and think I may have over-reacted a bit with the imminent death thing. Feeling much better today and reckon we're all going to live long and healthy lives.' Either way, whoever did write it got it badly wrong. Almost five thousand years later the world is still very much here, and, of course, just as degenerate, if not more so. And as for bribery and corruption . . .

2. The world will end in the 2nd century AD

This date for the total and utter annihilation of all humankind was predicted by one Montanus, a charismatic fellow who, after being converted to Christianity, travelled round preaching what he claimed was the word of God, as given to him personally by, erm, God.

On his travels he was accompanied by two women, Prisca and Maximilla, who also claimed the inspiration of the Holy Spirit, though it is strongly suspected that they received their divine words via Montanus' penis.

In AD 155 he founded his own sect and named its followers (in a lovely, entirely non-egotistical way) the Montanists. Montanus, well, God talking through Montanus, told his followers that Christ's return, and the accompanying end of the world, were imminent, so he ordered them to join him in Anatolia, Central Turkey to wait, arm-in-arm for the day of doom. 'Yeah', his followers might have been thinking, 'I've heard that one before'.

But here's the thing; back then, they hadn't really heard that one before. Old Monty had hit upon the formula for death cult leadership that has been followed by just about every death cult leader since. How his afterlife self must wish he'd copyrighted it.

Naturally, the world didn't end at the time described by

Monty, which enabled him to discover another aspect of death cult leadership, which is that incredibly, even after you've made yourself look like a complete and utter pillock, your followers remain loyal. (If you want to check out why this seemingly nonsensical state of affairs exists check out a book called *When Prophecy Fails*.)

Which is exactly what the Montanists did, continuing to spread his (utterly incorrect) word and founding a movement that lasted for another six centuries.

3. *The world will end in September 1186*

Causing widespread panic and chaos is a piece of cake these days, a click of a button is all it takes and thy will, will go viral. Back in the 12th century creating a Botnet army of computers wasn't an option, which makes the famed Toledo Letter all the more impressive, though only in the 'widespread panic' sense and not in the 'correctly predicting the end of the world' sense, as we shall see.

This document, believed to have been the work of a bunch of astrologers from the Spanish region of Toledo, or possibly just one called John, predicted that September 1186 would see our planet subjected to all manner of mayhem. Winds, storms, drought, famine, pestilence and earthquakes were foretold, along with a warning that the air would grow dark and men's hearts would be destroyed by a terrible voice. The letter advised people to flee from their homes sharpish and head for the mountains, ideally, one assumes, with a pair of earplugs in case the terrible voice should carry.

When some wag suggested sending it to Pope Clement III, the others agreed and not only did so, but also sent it off to other 'men of weight'.

In no time at all, in medieval terms, Europe was gripped by the aforementioned widespread panic with many a sound-proofed mountainside property being snapped up by the

gullible hordes. 'Head for the hills' became a religious instruc-
tion and thousands waited in terror for the winds and hail and
unpleasant rasping tones from above.

The letter even reached the Archbishop of Canterbury, one
Baldwin of Exeter who did what any good Archbishop would
do in the circumstances to prevent the ensuing apocalypse;
he ordered a three day fast. Yes, interesting how things have
changed. Nowadays, when told that we're all going to die, it's
generally accepted that the thing to do is have sex with the
nearest person, whereas some 850 years ago you were expected
to stop eating for 72 hours.

Needless to say September 1186 was a relatively uneventful
month, save for some people feeling hungrier than normal and
lots of folk getting chills on account of exposure to mountain
air.

Incredibly that wasn't the end of the Toledo Letter, not by a
long chalk. Since 1186 it has cropped up again on numerous
occasions with one crucial difference each time; the date for
the end of the world has been changed. So, in 1214 it popped
through the letter box of one Cardinal Johannes Toletanus
predicting 1229 as the year of Armageddon; in 1395 it found
its way to the Magisters of Paris, and in 1480 it either arrived
at, or was attributed to, a Mount Sinai Hermit, the Rasis of
Antiochia, though that might be two different people, and
reckoned it'd all be over by 1510. There are even some who say
that a version still exists today that predicts the end of the
world for 2012.

It has therefore taken on the form of a kind of world-ending
chain letter which can immediately be binned or utilised to set
up a new pyramid selling scam. No doubt it will still be doing
the rounds long after all of us are gone and in the year 3469
people will still be screaming on receiving it and making hasty
preparations for an escape to their nearest hillock.

4. The world will end in 1504-ish

For prophets of doom and gloom, the dawn of a new millennium is often a very busy time. Rather than welcome it in with gleeful optimism and excitement, these old miseries see it as a great opportunity to foretell un-gleeful death and destruction for all of us – putting many a downer on New Year's Eve celebrations.

In 1500 the party pooper was none other than Renaissance artist extraordinaire Sandro Botticelli who unleashed on to the world his Mystical Nativity painting. It's a cracking work, if you like that sort of thing, lots of pretty colours, nicely painted people and a bull, but what concerns us is an inscription Botticelli put at the top which reads . . .

> This picture, at the end of the year 1500, in the troubles of Italy, I Alessandro, in the half-time after the time, painted, according to the eleventh chapter of Saint John, in the second woe of the Apocalypse, during the release of the devil for three-and-a-half years; then he shall be bound in the twelfth chapter and we shall see him buried as in this picture.

No wonder he called it mystical, but those who had an inkling as to what he was banging on about reckoned that he was predicting the end of the world some time in 1504. He wasn't correct, in any shape or form or oil or canvas, and the effect of his arty prediction seems to have been minimal beyond someone saying, 'I think you've made Joseph's ears a bit too big.'

Today of course Botticelli is revered as a great master and has also kindly given his name to a guessing game, but more importantly, his works sell for a fortune – in 2006 his Madonna and Child sold for $7.5 million – something he probably wishes he had predicted so that he could have seen his descendants all right for a few bob.

5. The world will end on 1 February 1524

It's always nice to be presented with a specific date for end-of-the-world predictions and our first was unleashed by a bunch of 16th century astrologers. Astrology was big business in 1520s London with some cunning proponents even making a living by writing horoscopes in newspapers (astrological predictions in a newspaper? Why the hell did they think that would ever catch on?).

So when a distinguished group of Renaissance Russell Grants got together in June 1523 and – having looked at the planets, their charts and quite probably the bottom of a few tankards of mead – predicted that the world would end on 1 February the following year, they were taken, really quite seriously. The astrologers calculated that on this date the River Thames would overflow, marking the start of the second Great Flood, or first if you don't believe in the biblical one. Remarkably, because of this prediction, no less than 20,000 people moved out of London in the ensuing months.

No doubt inner city property prices plummeted and well apportioned Thameside apartments were snapped up by canny astrologers because come the fateful day, yes, you've guessed it, nothing happened. It didn't even bleeding well rain, which for February in the UK, is pretty remarkable.

The following day the astrologers regrouped and came up with a brilliant excuse as to why their prediction had gone wrong; they'd miscalculated by a hundred years. They should have said 1624 instead of 1524, by which time they'd of course be dead and therefore wouldn't be around to hear anyone berate them for screwing things up.

Interestingly though, the original prediction still stands as one of the most accurate ever made using astrological methods.

6. The world will end on 19 May 1719

So far, the apocalyptical predictions have been based on someone being a bit depressed, religion and astrology, and thus you might feel there is a sound basis for them being complete bollocks. However, though Science may offer up carefully calculated predictions of our demise which are based on solid principles, it really is no less deserving of derision for the simple reason that, they too, are complete bollocks.

One of the first to besmirch his good name in such a way was famed Swiss mathematician Jacob Bernoulli who, in 1681 published the nattily titled, *Newly discovered Method of how the path of a Comet or Tailed Star can be reduced to certain fundamental laws, and its appearance predicted.* Surprisingly, it wasn't the bestseller that Jacob had hoped for, despite the fact it included a prediction that on 19 May 1719 The Great Comet would return with divinely inspired, earth-shattering consequences. (For those of a non-astronomical bent, Jacob was talking about the Great Comet of 1680, also known as Kirch's Comet or C/1680 V1 which at one point was only 898,000 km away from Earth, perilously close in comet terms apparently.)

The following year, possibly due to the book's lack of success, old Jakey hit upon the brilliant idea of re-releasing it, only this time, in Latin with the far more enticing title, *Conamen novi systematis cometarum pro motu eorum sub calculum revocando de apparitionibus praecedendis adornatum.* In this version he repeated his prediction, but with one subtle difference; this time he claimed it was only the comet's tail, and not its body, that was a sign of divine wrath. It was a brilliant new plot twist, but incredibly the book still couldn't crack the top ten, so Jacob went back to being a mathematician, and a rather good one at that.

He died in 1705, which was a shame because had he lived he would have discovered that 19 May 1719 was a lovely, comet-free spring day, and his scientist mates could all have had a good laugh at his expense.

7. The world will end in 1806

When someone who is known to be a thief and con artist starts making predictions about the end of the world, the chances of her being taken seriously should really be zero. Ah, if only. In 1806 a hen belonging to one such known thief and con artist, Mary Bateman of Leeds, produced a most incredible egg. Not a golden one, rather one with the words, 'Christ is coming' on it.

Astounded by her poultry prophet, instead of asking it who was going to win the 3:30 at Ascot that day, Mary took the egg and showed it to the locals. The locals may have been wary of Mary's honesty rating and probably kept a close eye on their shawl pockets but they were taken in by what this smooth-talking grifter showed them and piled back to her house where she announced to the amassed throng that she'd had a message from God; in it he'd told her that the foretelling fowl would lay 14 such eggs in total, after which the world would come to an abrupt end.

Right on cue another one popped out at which point Mary went on to say that God had also, very kindly, revealed to her how everyone could be saved from the approaching apocalypse, and, for the very reasonable fee of only one penny she would pass on the death-avoiding method. This is the point you might have thought that people would see through the very thin veneer of wool being pulled over their eyes and take their leave, but no, they duly paid their penny and waited expectantly.

Mary then moved on to the next stage of her long con and revealed that, in order to be saved, they needed a specially sealed piece of paper with the letters, 'J.C.' written on it, a number of which she just happened to have available for the knock down price of just one shilling.

Guess what? The suckers forked out again and over the next few days as the hen continued to produce more magically inscribed eggs, crowds flocked to Mary's house to stump up their hard-earned in return for a slice of salvation until, after the 14th egg had been laid, the world miraculously ... stayed very firmly in place and Mary was nicked.

Three years later she came to a very predictable end when she was hanged for fraud and murder, after which her body was put on public display and strips of skin from it were sold as charms to ward of evil spirits. It's a classic case of the long con transforming into a dead con.

8. *The world will end on 25 December 1814*

Joanna Southcott was the daughter of a farmer who, until the age of 42, worked as a domestic servant in Exeter. Then, for reasons that remain unknown but are thought to be 'because she went bonkers', she became a religious prophetess.

Starting slowly, she eventually began pulling out the big guns and her coup de grace was delivered at the age of 64 when she predicted that on 25 December 1814, despite the fact that she was a virgin, she would give birth to the new Christ-child and the end of days would begin. If only someone had explained the facts of life to her, though to be fair, there is a precedent for that sort of thing.

That Christmas she did begin to experience something akin to labour pains, but it was later put down to a dodgy mince pie, and no newborn, Christ-like or otherwise, was forthcoming. Unfortunately for Joanna, something else pretty significant did occur on that day; she died. If only she'd predicted that it was to be the end of her days, and not bothered with that bit about the Christ-child, she would have been spot on.

However, in spite of her prediction not coming true in any way at all, a group of Southcott devotees mourned her passing and claimed she had been a person with truly magical powers of insight (unlike them). Astoundingly, her status increased over the years mainly due to a mysterious box that she left behind, un-astoundingly and un-mysteriously known as 'Joanna Southcott's Box'.

The box apparently contained sure-fire prophecies and was only to be opened at a time of national crisis in the presence of 24 bishops of the Church of England. In fact it was finally prised open in 1927 in the presence of one reluctant prelate and found to contain a lottery ticket, and not even a winning one.

Incredibly, Southcott's followers, or as some call them, 'the most gullible people on Earth', claimed that the box that had been opened was not the real one. That, apparently, is in the possession of a group calling themselves The Panacea Society and, as recently as the 1960s and 70s, they placed adverts in the *Sunday Express* newspaper to try and persuade 24 bishops of its importance and to attend the opening. Despite the power of advertising, they failed, though the bishops who read the paper *were* convinced by another advert to try the new men's aftershave Hi Karate.

9. The world will end on or before 1844. Okay, more specifically, some time between 21 March 1843 and 21 March 1844. No, silly me, I meant, 18 April 1844, by which I actually mean 22 October 1844

This classic example from the, 'if at first you don't succeed, try, try again' school of prediction is the work of William Miller, an American preacher, who, despite being wrong, wrong, wrong and wrong is generally credited with starting a movement, the Millerites, which in turn led, directly or indirectly, to the creation of many other religious groupings such as Seventh-Day Adventists, Advent Christians and Jehovah's Witnesses.

His first pronouncement came in September 1822 when, after many years of bible study he said:

I believe that the second coming of Jesus Christ is near, even at the door, even within twenty-one years, on or before 1844.

Unfortunately, Miller neglected to say whose door he was talking about, which led to many of his followers keeping their doors in pristine condition for the next 21 years, just in case.

Of course, 'on or before 1844' is frankly a bit woolly, there are a lot of preparations to be made if the world is going to end and Jesus is returning to take us all off to heaven – there are sandwiches to be made and knapsacks to be prepared. So pressed to be more specific he proclaimed,

My principles in brief, are, that Jesus Christ will come again to this earth, cleanse, purify, and take possession of the same, with all the saints, sometime between March 21, 1843, and March 21, 1844.

Still on the woolly side of not woolly, but marginally better, though only in terms of sandwich making and not in terms of accuracy, as most people realised on 22 March 1844.

Obviously the problem was one of simple miscalculation and, after a quick reassessment of the texts, a new date of 18 April 1844 was given. Now that was more like it, all woolliness banished and people could plan properly for the big day, some are even believed to have ordered plentiful supplies of egg and cress in expectation. The only minor problem, just a glitch really, occurred when 18 April came and went without even the briefest appearance of the messiah.

To be fair to Mr Miller, he did acknowledge his mistake, writing,

I confess my error, and acknowledge my disappointment; yet I still believe that the day of the Lord is near, even at the door.

That was big of him, but before you could say, 'you're just

making it all up aren't you?' another date had been set, 22 October 1844. Among Millerites this day became known as the Great Disappointment, for reasons which we won't insult your intelligence by explaining.

Astoundingly, some of Miller's followers actually gave up their beliefs after the GD, but others were less hasty and interpreted his complete and utter failure in different ways, leading to various splinter groups forming which are still around today and whose followers number in their millions.

Rarely can failure have been quite so successful.

10. The world will end in 1874/1882/1892/1911/1914

The Great Pyramid of Giza is one of the wonders of the world; it's an incredible feat of engineering and big respect is due to the ancient Egyptians for all that toil and precision engineering. It was built around 2560 BC and remained largely free of upstarts trying to make a name for themselves until 1859 when John Taylor published a book on it containing some mathematical theories about the pyramid's design, along with a claim that it was the work of none other than Noah – the ark chap from the bible.

The book was read by Charles Piazzi Smith, at the time the Astronomer Royal for Scotland, who, rather than put it in the bin, thought it quite good and decided to head off to Egypt and investigate for himself.

Five years later Smith produced his own book, which completely knocked John's into touch. In it he claimed that the architects of the pyramid could only have been directed by the hand of God and, that it was full of prophecies that could be revealed by certain measurements. The prophecies, he said, had to be worked out using a special measurement called the pyramid inch, so, naturally, he got his ruler out and started prophesising. (Fantastically, he also proposed another measurement called the pyramid pint. Three of them and before you know it, you're up on the table, naked and singing 'Walk Like An Egyptian'.) According to Smith's pyramidal calculations the world was going to end in either 1882, 1892 or 1911.

Not so according to Nelson Barbour and Charles Russell, the founding fathers of the Jehovah's Witness movement, who were curiously influenced by his book and, using Smith's methods, came up with either 1874 or 1914.

All utter nonsense, of course, as the non-destruction of the world in any of those years clearly proved. However, that hasn't stopped others making similar prophecies since, and indeed other mystical claims for the great pyramid, which to this day has refused to comment, preferring instead to distance itself from such matters and stand serenely in the noonday sun posting haughty glances at the hordes of tourists scrambling over themselves to capture it on cheap digital cameras.

11. The world will end on 20 May 1910

As has been observed, comets are pretty high up on the list of things that might bring about the end of the world, and when it comes to these enormous celestial speed freaks the numero uno, the Daddy, the king of them all, is of course Halley's Comet. It swings by for a visit roughly every 75 years giving plenty of scope for doomsmiths to spread their gospel of oblivion every time it does so.

On 20 May 1910 big H was due to pass pretty close by, but, more importantly, its course meant that the earth was going to pass right through its tail. No biggee you might think, but then, this was no ordinary tail. This was a 40 million kilometre long tail made up of cosmic dust no less. So when, in February 1910, Chicago's Yerkes Observatory let it be known that they had detected the gas cyanogen in it, well, all that was needed was for someone to give the tiniest of nudges and pandemonium would surely break out.

That person was French astronomer Camille Flammarion

who, it was reported in the *New York Times*, claimed that
cyanogen,

> would impregnate the atmosphere and possibly snuff out all life
> on the planet.

Despite hedging his bets by the use of that time-honoured get-out word – 'possibly' – the damage was done. Panic ensued in a number of US cities with people buying up gas masks by the truckloads as well as 'comet pills'.

Yes, never one to miss an opportunity, a number of business-minded citizens, or crooks as they're otherwise known, saw the end of the world as a great money-making opportunity and produced these pills that they claimed could counter the effects of cyanogen. Whether they could or not was largely immaterial as on the appointed day Earth miraculously survived the tail to tell the tale, an event joyfully reported in the *Chicago Tribune* under the headline, 'We're Still Here'.

Unfortunately for Flammarion, he was too, and both he and comet pill sellers presumably kept the shutters closed that day … and for many days to come.

12. *The world will end on 10 March 1982*

From the haughty and slightly patronising perspective of the 21st century, a 16th century scientist incorrectly predicting the end of the world is eminently understandable and forgivable, rather sweet in fact, bless his little cotton socks. Similarly, although slightly more advanced, getting it wrong at the beginning of the 20th century is also understandable. But when two Cambridge educated astrophysicists make a similar cataclysmic error in the latter part of the 20th century however, there really is no hiding place.

In 1974, said Cambridge educated astrophysicists, John Gribbin and Stephen Plagemann wrote a book called *The Jupiter*

Effect in which they predicted that an alignment of planets on 10 March 1982 would basically create mayhem on Earth. All manner of cosmic events were foretold such as floods, earthquakes and volcanic eruptions, though, strangely, not massive personal and professional embarrassment. The book was a bestseller and as the date of doom approached observatories around the world were bombarded with phone calls from concerned citizens.

And they were right to be concerned because on that day in March high tides were recorded as being a whopping 40 micrometres, or forty millionth of a metre, higher than the average for that time of year. Alternatively, in more scientific terms, bugger all happened.

Faced with the observable reality of their epic mistake, Gribbin and Plagemann did what any honourable person would do; they wrote another book called *The Jupiter Effect Reconsidered*. It's a very short tome containing just the one page on which is written the words, 'Sorry, we got it wrong'. Actually, it was considerably longer and tried to explain where they had gone wrong the first time round, which was basically not to shut up about their ridiculous theory.

The good news for the Cambridge educated astrophysicists is that the follow up book also sold well leading to an incredible career as a writer for John Gribbin in particular, who has subsequently written over a hundred books, though to date none of them have been called, *There's Cash in Cataclysm*.

13. The world will end at one second past midnight on 1 January 2000

What makes this prediction unique is that there isn't really anyone to pin it on other than the computer industry or technology experts, so despite an obscene amount of money being spent on apparently making sure the world didn't end at that time, there's no single individual to really blame and rip the living piss out of.

This is, of course, the Millennium Bug or Y2K as it is annoyingly acronised (Year Two Thousand if you're wondering). Essentially, so the story went, because computers only used two digits to signify the year instead of four (95 instead of 1995 for instance), when their clocks toppled over from 1999 into 2000 they wouldn't be able to cope and havoc would be wreaked.

It was a terrifying prospect and, rather than do their utmost to quell the flames of panic, there were many who poured petrol on this rapidly spreading fire. Helpfully, Senator Robert F. Bennett, chair of the Senate Special Committee on the Year 2000 Technology Problem, said,

> When people say to me, 'Is the world going to come to an end?'
> I say, 'I don't know.'

Not wanting to miss out on all the scaremongering his colleague John Hamre, America's Deputy Secretary of Defense at the time, proclaimed that,

> The Y2K problem is the electronic equivalent of the El Niño and there will be nasty surprises around the globe.

(El Niño is a climate pattern that causes floods, droughts and other nasty, world-ending type things.)

Meanwhile, the *New York Times* went with,

> A global financial crash, nuclear meltdowns, hospital life support system shutdowns, a collapse of the air-traffic system are possible without proper attention now.

Elsewhere there were warnings of nuclear war, economic chaos, food shortages and the possibility of aeroplanes falling out of the sky. Consequently, an awful lot of preventative work was done in the run up to the new millennium and, as anyone who has ever paid to have their computer fixed or spent hours trying to do so by talking to a geek on the end of a premium rate phone line knows, tech-heads don't come cheap. In total it is estimated that, brace yourselves, over $300 billion dollars was spent trying to fix the problem.

That's a lot of money and no mistake, but the world didn't end as the new millennium dawned, so presumably it was money well spent.

Weeeeeeelllll, that's a moot point, you see; there are some who call the whole Y2K problem the, 'hoax of the century' and back up their argument by pointing out the following: Very few American schools did anything about the millennium bug, yet they experienced no problems at all. Similarly, about 1.5 million businesses did nothing and they were also fine. Quite a few countries did very little to tackle the problem and all of them still exist today. The 2000 financial year began much earlier in 1999 and yet there were no problems caused by computers belonging to financial institutions when it started. It's all water under the bridge now, or $300 billion under the bridge to be exact, but it is just possible that Y2K was in fact ALOOB; a load of old bollocks.

How the myriad of companies set up to deal with Y2K must have been rubbing their hands in the run up to 31 December 1999 and how they must have enjoyed their first class, perfectly safe flights to Venezuela on 1 January 2000, with their accompanying bags of cash.

14. The world will end when the Large Hadron Collider accidentally makes a black hole and we're all sucked into it

The Large Hadron Collider is the biggest and best particle accelerator in the world. It can hurl protons at each other faster than any other of its ilk and in so doing could recreate the big bang and answer some of life's most fundamental questions, such as, why do birds suddenly appear every time you are near? Unfortunately, in doing so, it might also bring about the end of the world, a somewhat delicious irony in that just as we find out what it's all about, *it* gets blown to smithereens.

The two main concerns seem to be that firstly the LHD might create micro black holes which could expand, thus becoming presumably, bleeding enormous great black holes, and therefore catastrophic; and, secondly, that it could create strangelets, complicated things which are difficult to explain for scientific lightweights such as ourselves, but suffice to say, they could do something really bad as well.

Such was the level of concern at one time that some people filed lawsuits to try and prevent physicists switching the LHD on, which, when reported, led to some very responsible journalism such as that found in the *Sun* under the headline, 'End of the World Due in 9 Days', and the *Daily Mail* whose headline read, 'Are We All Going To Die Next Wednesday?'

Scientists responded with slightly fewer hysterical articles such as 'Astrophysical implications of hypothetical stable TeV-scale black holes' and 'Study of Potentially Dangerous Events During Heavy-Ion Collisions at the LHC', which, while not being so hot on eye-catching headlines, basically concluded that there was, and still is, nothing at all to worry about.

Or is there? (No.)

15. The world will end on 21 December 2012

Currently in End of the World circles the clever money is on the above date because it is the end date of some Mayan calendar cycle. The Mayans were a proud people from Central America with, by all accounts, quite an advanced culture which was somewhat screwed up by the Spanish, but quite what they did to deserve all this attention is not really clear.

You could say, 'well, so what if their calendar cycle ends

on 21 December 2012, big whoopee', which would be a very understandable and rational standpoint, if a little flippant, but others would be quick to point out the error of your ways.

Many theories abound as to what is actually going to happen on that date. Some say there is going to be a change in the orientation of the earth's magnetic field or geomagnetic reversal, which would create energy equivalent to 100 billion atomic bombs; while others harp on about planetary alignments causing black holes and attracting loads of comets. Then there's a claim that a planet known as Nibiru is going to come smashing into the earth in a sort of celestial game of conkers, so, just in case, perhaps we should douse the planet in vinegar to harden it up. Finally, for the time being, aliens are apparently on their way and set to invade on that date. Presumably this information has come from a mole in the alien organisation, or a human being working deep undercover.

All very worrying, though not really as it's codswallop of the highest order.

Mayan people today are not in the least bit concerned about 21 December 2012 and scientists have reassured people that none of the predicted planetary alignments and suchlike are going to happen. In fact, the advice is to carry on buying Christmas presents as normal that year, such as this book, which would make the perfect gift for anyone and won't cost the earth.

16. The world will end in about five billion years, give or take three to four billion years, though it might not happen

This, in a nutshell of sorts, is what science currently says. Essentially, so the theory goes, at some point in the future, our wonderful sun, the very same sun that comes out on lovely bright days, will start to expand (please don't ask why, it's something to do with gases) and enter what is known as its 'Red Giant Phase'. Now, some among you might argue that the sun is already pretty 'giant' and thus it should really just be called, its 'Red Phase', but ignoring you pedants for a moment, at one time it was fairly widely agreed in the scientific community that the process would start some five billion years hence.

Once this expansion has started, it's going to get hot, really, really hot. So hot that not even factor 50 will protect you. In short, Earth will burn to a crisp, or melt to a fondue or dissipate like a … OK, you get the picture. Whatever happens, it's a pretty terrifying prospect for our great, great, great, great, great … x 333 million grandchildren.

Recently, however, some scientists have recalculated and estimated that the expansion will begin about three months from now. No, only kidding; the new estimate for the sun to get ever more giant is in about one to two billion years. Either way, it's really not worth worrying about, unless you're reading a copy of this book in the year 1,000,002,011 (in which case, the book has stood the test of time and spent millions of weeks in the bestseller charts, or it has been discovered by an archaeologist and is kept in a museum somewhere as an example of an early 21st century holy scripture).

But, there's even less reason to worry because *it might not happen*. In 2007 the good folk at Italy's National Institute of Astrophysics discovered that a planet similar (ish) to Earth had astonishingly survived its sun's red giant phase. How? Well, rather than being fried, the planet, nattily named V391 Pegasi b, was simply pushed into an orbit twice as far away from its sun, presumably giving it another couple of billion years before the same thing happens again. If there had been any intelligent life forms on V391 Pegasi b, they would surely have celebrated long into the night, which, with their new position in the galaxy, now lasts twice as long. It's a win-win situation.

So, according to science it is toast or relocation an awfully long time from now.

JUST PLAIN RIDICULOUS

All of the predictions in this book are wrong, either partially or in their entirety. If they weren't, they'd be in another book about predictions that turned out right, in which case you might not have bought it, in which case your life would be slightly altered and you might not have met the man or woman of your dreams in the bookshop, instead ending up lonely, bitter and destitute. (Good job you bought this book then eh?)

It's easy to laugh at thinkers from the past who made those mistakes though, they had none of the knowledge we possess. Some of their mistakes are completely understandable in a non-patronising historically empathetic way. For example, when cars were first invented, it's perfectly reasonable that someone could feel compelled to forecast that they'd never take the place of bicycles; two wheels good, four wheels bad.

But if someone had a rush of blood to the head and, for no apparent reason, predicted that humans would one day be able to digest the cellulose in grass and in the future, herds of homo sapiens would be seen grazing in meadows, that wouldn't be completely understandable; that would be completely and plainly ridiculous. You see where we're going with this one. ...

1. Inredibly Uirky

This chapter wouldn't be complete without a contribution from our good friend John Elfreth Watkins Jr and thankfully he has supplied us with a corker. As you may recall John spoke to some of the *'most learned minds'* and *'the wisest and most careful of men'* in order to compile his list of predictions for the year 2000, as recorded in the *Ladies Home Journal* of 1900. There are 29 in total and plonked more or less in the middle is this really quite remarkable claim.

There will be no C, X or Q in our every-day alphabet.

Er, and why not?

They will be abandoned because unnecessary.

Unnecessary? That's so absurd it's worth repeating. Unnecessary? At a push, and really quite a big one, it's possible to see why Q and X might seem unnecessary, though Ueen Victoria might have had something to say about that, to say nothing of ylophone and jack-in-the-bo manufacturers, but C?

Of the two letters with that sound, which some parents distinguish between by calling one curly and the other kicking, surely the far less used and far less versatile, K, should be the one to go? Apart from the odd few occasions when it's silent and thus barely necessary itself, it has just one sound, whereas C is a multi-talented letter as the words coelosphaerium and astrophysicist will testify.

What about Z? Okay, it's ten points in scrabble, but how necessary is it really? So we'd lose zip, hazy and zebra, and some words for chemical compounds maybe such as cyclo-piazonic acid, but no one would really shed a tear if it went would they?

What about the last in, first out rule? In Old English there used to be letters known as 'thorn' and 'wynn', which eventually became 'y' and 'w'. Surely, if any letters should go it should be them? But we don't want any letters to go. Apart from anything else, losing C, Q and X would screw up the alphabet song. Go on, sing it, it's hard enough getting past B.

Tempting as it is to label John 'a omplete ok' though, let's desist and continue on with the rest of his prediction.

> Spelling by sound will have been adopted, first by the newspapers. English will be a language of condensed words expressing condensed ideas, and will be more extensively spoken than any other. Russian will rank second.

Watkins Junior did have a point. The irregularities of the English language are maddening at the best of times – try telling a child you've just taught the letter sounds 't' 'h' and 'e' about the word 'the'. They'd either burst out crying or deck you one. Furthermore, it's probable that back in 1900 kids learnt whole words parrot fashion rather than by focusing on the individual letter sounds, but quite why and how newspapers should first adopt this approach is not at all clear.

As for English being the most spoken language, well, it's currently second to Mandarin with Russian fifth or sixth depending on who's doing the counting, but, a language of condensed words expressing condensed ideas? What exactly is a condensed idea? Is that the same as a half-baked notion? Or, like its cousin condensed milk, is it a particularly thick, sweet and sickly idea?

Ultimately it seems that, extrapolating John's prediction, if it was correct, by the year 3000 we would have condensed ideas so much that only the basics such as eat, sleep, shit and shag would need to be expressed and then only through the medium of mime.

2. Don't interrupt me, I'm flying

The following rather interesting prediction was made in the February 1950 edition of *Popular Mechanics* magazine in an article entitled, 'Miracles You'll See In The Next Fifty Years'.

By the year 2000 aerial travel will never be interrupted.

On its own it's quite an odd claim to make, but fear not, there is some very un-sound reasoning behind it. With somewhat startling specificity the magazine says that at some point in the years preceding 2000 a Dr Vladimir Zworykin and a Dr John Van Neumann will create a machine that is able to predict the weather with, as they put it, '*an accuracy unattainable before 1980*'.

It's a very rare example of a prediction not just about a future invention, but about the people who will actually invent it, meaning that it's a prediction that is wrong on two counts, or, put more simply, very, very wrong.

Although Zworykin, an inventor, engineer and pioneer of television technology, and Neumann, a mathematician, did work on electronic weather forecasting together, Neumann, entirely unpredictably, died in 1957, by which time many believe their research had progressed to the point whereby they could confidently predict that if it looks overcast, it might rain a bit, and if a few rays of sunshine are cutting through the clouds, shorts and a t-shirt might be a better clothing option than top to toe body warmers.

Who knows what might have happened had Neumann lived, though by 1980, the year the magazine implies that the invention was going to be ready, he would have been 77, and Zworykin was 92 (he died in 1982), so the chances are they'd probably have thought, 'sod this for a lark, I'd rather have a chocolate digestive and a little nap'.

Having stuck its neck out though, the article goes on to

explain that the weather machine will be used to spot *'budding hurricanes in the doldrums off the coast of Africa'*. All fine and dandy, but once spotted, what next for Hurricane Zworykin? Well, according to the magazine,

> ... before it has a chance to gather much strength and speed as it travels westward toward Florida, oil is spread over the sea and ignited. There is an updraft. Air from the surrounding region, which includes the developing hurricane, rushes into fill the void. The rising air condenses so that some of the water in the whirling mass falls as rain.

Yes, unbelievably, deep within this conglomeration of gobbledygook they have somehow managed to accurately predict that a huge amount of oil will one day appear near Florida. The somewhat crucial difference being though, that the more recent spillage was an accident, whereas the idea back in 1950 was to purposely cover the ocean with oil. Oh, and then set fire to it. Clearly, in those days an environmental catastrophe was less important than some early package holidaymakers getting their two weeks in the sun.

So, having laid out its cast iron scientific theory, the magazine feels fully justified in delivering its prediction by saying, *'With storms diverted where they do no harm, aerial travel is never interrupted'*. And of course they are absolutely right because once all the oceans have dried up, all aquatic life becomes extinct and acid rain, caused by burning oil, has destroyed the forests, there won't be much of a planet left, leaving Zworykin and Neumann, who will no doubt have been cryogenically frozen, to re-emerge and fly around uninterrupted to their hearts' content.

3. *Vacuum up the mess, but don't get too near the hoover*

At the end of World War Two, the world was treated to a demonstration of nuclear power that most saw as a shocking example of the most evil form of evil, which really is quite terribly evil.

Some, however, looked within the mushroom cloud and saw something else; a business opportunity. One such person was Alex Lewyt whose company, the Lewyt Corporation, spent the war involved in the vital service of manufacturing vacuum products for the Navy – perhaps they'd intended them to be used for sucking up enemy submarines. After the war Lewyt's company made quite a lot of loot in the vacuum cleaner market, but competition was fierce and he needed to find a way of standing out from the crowd, something that would get him and, by association, his company, noticed. The opportunity reared its head in 1955 when the *New York Times* came knocking and Alex duly supplied them with a sound bite.

> Nuclear powered vacuum cleaners will probably be a reality within ten years.

That's one way to blow the competition out of the water, and the universe, assuming you put the nuclear powered vacuum cleaner on the correct setting of course. In one fell swoop he'd managed to make a tedious, but relatively safe household chore into a terrifying, life threatening household chore. Granted, in one almighty suck you might be able to hoover up all the dust in your house, and your entire neighbourhood, but you'd have to wear 15 layers of protective clothing and, once you'd finished, put the bag in a sealed metal container and bury it 300 feet below ground for a least 20,000 years, which frankly, is a bit of a faff.

A housewife in the mid-Sixties as predicted by Alex Lewyt.

Sadly Mr Lewyt didn't get to see whether his prediction came true; not because he stood too close to an experimental model and grew three extra ears and another nose, on his elbow, but because just five years later he sold his business to the Shetland Floor Polisher Company who, for some strange reason, didn't share his vision.

In more recent times scientists have continued to develop nuclear energy, but surprisingly they've overlooked its usage in the vacuuming industry and focused more on creating electricity and preventing environmental disasters caused by meltdowns.

4. Car Chameleon

While not, perhaps, an overriding concern when buying a car, the choice of colour can cause consternation. Should you go for the silver or the blue Roller? It's not easy. Colour says a lot about a person and even the wrong shade or tone can make the difference between classy and twatty.

Just such a terrible quandary was clearly at the forefront of the minds of those working in the automobile industry in the late Fifties and, according to our old chum Arthur Radebaugh, a breakthrough was imminent.

> The automobile industry is studying a new kind of specially sensitive car body finish whose color can be changed at will. An electromagnetic gun would emit rays that would instantly 'repaint' the car in any desired hue or combination, perhaps to harmonize with milady's new fall outfit.

It really does conjure up a marvellous image of milady who, having spent hours getting herself ready to go out, demands migentleman turn round and go back home to re-colour micar because it doesn't go with her scarf.

Of course, criminals would also have a field day. 'Calling all cars, calling all cars, be on the look out for a green Ford Fiesta ... no, sorry, a yellow Fiesta ... actually, it's white ...'

But that's not all. This wonderful new technology could do much more than just change a car's colour. Well, it could do one other thing as well apparently.

> D.S. Harder, retired executive vice-president at Ford, recently described research in this direction. He added that this new kind of 'photosensitive' surface would also be self-cleaning, with the silent energy of static electricity or a supersonic vibrator driving off all dust and dirt.

How both milady and migentleman must be rejoicing yet more. He gets to spend Sunday mornings lounging in bed instead of cleaning the car, and she gets to spend Sunday mornings lounging in bed with a supersonic vibrator.

Sadly the research mentioned by Delmar, for that is the

'D' in D.S. Harder, must have headed off in a different direction leaving milady and migentleman with a non-colour changing, non-self-cleaning car, and quite probably, a non-marriage.

5. All shook up

There's an aura about certain people that screams, 'this person is going places'. Sometimes you can just tell that greatness has entered the room. Then again, there are days when your greatness radar is faulty and seems to have accidentally gone into reverse mode.

Jimmy Denny could well have been having one of those days on 2 October 1954. At the time he was the manager of country music venue Grand Old Opry in Nashville, Tennessee who took a chance on a new, young performer called Elvis Presley.

By all accounts it wasn't Elvis' best gig with reports suggesting the audience reacted 'politely' to his gyrations, which is more than could be said for Jimmy, whose prediction for Elvis, along with some thoughtful and constructive advice, was as follows:

> You ain't going nowhere son. You ought to go back to driving a truck.

Elvis no doubt left the building on this occasion without anyone taking a blind bit of notice, but it was probably just that sort of keen insight which, the following year, saw Jimmy named *Billboard* magazine's Country and Western Man of the Year and, three years after his death in 1963, helped him get elected into the Country Music Hall of Fame.

As for the Elvis fella, no one is quite sure what became of him.

6. *Horseshit in all senses of the word (which is in fact just the two)*

One of the great facets of us human beings is that more often than not when the answer to a problem is staring us right slap bang in the face we somehow manage not to see it and instead predict dire consequences due to said problem.

A glorious instance of this occurred towards the end of the 19th century. The problem was horses. Or, to be more precise their bottoms. Or, to be as precise as it's possible to be in this case, the solid-ish matter that came out of their bottoms.

At the time horses were very much the preferred mode of transport and, in cities such as London and New York that meant there were an awful lot of them. Estimates for London put the number of equines in the city each day at 60,000 plus, while New York welcomed about 100,000 nags daily. Given that your average gee gee produces between 15 and 35 pounds of poo poo a day that added up to really quite a lot of pony, the prospect of which was scaring some people shitless.

It really was a mare, so much so that in 1894 *The Times* of London predicted that by 1950 the entire city would be buried under 9 feet of cack, while New York's citizens were told that by 1930 they could look forward to horsey excrement rising up to third floor windows in Manhattan. That's way beyond knee deep in shit, not to mention the pong. If nothing was done the shit would not just hit the fan, but completely cover it, so in 1898 delegates at the first international urban planning conference gathered in New York to grapple with the mucky problem.

Here were the world's foremost experts in such matters, great minds who, individually, had no doubt solved many a taxing issue, but now, for the first time ever had come together. Surely the massive weight of their combined intellect would find a path through all the stallion shit. Perhaps the answer involved corks. Maybe there was a way of reducing the turd mountain by constipating the horses. Could the trotters even be trained to trot to a toilet if they had the trots?

Well, astoundingly, the delegates' efforts were frankly shit and, even though the conference had been planned to run for ten days, they gave up defeated and all went home after just three days. Not one of the so-called experts could foresee a future where the horse-powered automobile took over from the horse-powered horse as the main mode of transport, thus solving the problem in an instant, and, of course, creating another one, but let's not go there right now.

Pathetic. Frankly it would have served them right if they had all ended up buried under a huge mound of horsey do.

7. And from somewhere or other will come some bloke. He will say some things that are sort of about the future. They will be very vague and open to interpretation. Yet his influence will be huge among the gullible hordes from the West

It wouldn't really be right to have a book like this and not mention old Nostradamus. Some might say his predictions were far from hopeless, while others would argue that they were tosh in the extreme. The point, though, is that we just don't bloody know because they're so un-bloody-clear, and that's not due to the fact that originally they were in French and some other languages. Consequently, they are pretty hopeless. And extremely annoying.

Michel de Nostredame was born in France in 1503 and was basically a chemist, though he dabbled with becoming a doctor, and failed. He began making prophecies in 1550 by writing an almanac – probably to earn an extra franc or two – which proved so successful, spurred on by the great good he was doing, and definitely not by the cash, he decided to write some more. By the time he'd finished he'd notched up thousands, all written using slightly obscure language poems called quatrains, some rhyming, some not rhyming.

To be fair to Nossie, it was a bit of a tricky time to be doing such a thing; he didn't want to be called a heretic and carted off to a dungeon somewhere, so he had to be a wee bit careful, hence, apparently the somewhat ambiguous nature of his work.

That said, one of his most famous predictions is supposed to have been about Hitler.

> The two greatest ones of Asia and of Africa,
> From the Rhine and Lower Danube they will be said to have come,
> Cries, tears at Malta and the Ligurian side.

Where is Adolf then? Well, it turns out that Nostradamus used Latin when writing about the Danube, and in Latin it translates as Hister. Or in some interpretations, Ister. So it seems he was talking about a river and not a little Austrian bloke, though it's an easy mistake to make, they are very similar. Clearly it's unclear, but back in 1550 wouldn't it have been just as unclear to have said, 'From the Rhine and the Lower Danube will come a shouty man with distinctive hair on his upper lip?' No one back then would have had the foggiest what he was on about and he'd have been safe from the religious mobs, but we would have had a lot more to go on.

The other point about Michel's predictions is that they're only really ever interpreted in hindsight in a sort of, 'oh, now we know what he was on about, what a shame we didn't suss it out before September the 11th' way. That said though, it's unlikely a wholescale evacuation of New York would have been carried out if someone had rung up the police on 10 September and said, 'Look, Nostradamus wrote,

> at forty five degrees the sky will burn, fire to approach the great new city, in an instant a great scattered flame will leap up, when one will want to demand proof of the Normans.

'Can't you see? It's obvious, you've got to get everyone out of the city before it's too late!'

Another quatrain that is often held up as proof of Nossie's brilliance is the one in which he apparently predicts the moon landings.

> He will come to travel to the corner of Luna,
> where he will be captured and put in a strange land,
> The unripe fruits to be subject of great scandal,
> great blame, to one, great praise.

Here's how The Nostradamus Society of America interpret it.

He (*referring to mankind and the American Astronauts*) will come to travel to the corner of Luna (*the Moon*) where he will be captured (*on film*) and put into a strange land (*outer space and/or the Moon*). The unripe fruits (*assets which take time to develop before reaching maturity, a reference to the space race*), to be subjects of great scandal (*a reference to the Apollo One tragedy, the Challenger disaster, and other space related accidents*). Great blame (*to unnamed parties*) to one great praise (*a reference to the United States of America*).

Whereas it's possible to interpret it this way.

He (*referring to any member of The Nostradamus Society of America*) will come to travel to the corner of Luna (*will be thought of by sane people as a complete lunatic*), where he will be captured (*sectioned*) and put in a strange land (*psychiatric ward*). The unripe fruits (*on the ward he'll be served food that has not been properly prepared*) to be subjects of great scandal (*this will be leaked to the press after he gets very bad diarrhoea and tells a journalist*). Great blame (*after a lengthy legal battle the hospital in question will be found culpable*), to one great praise (*and he will be very happy with his lawyer who has got him millions in damages*).

At the end of the day, by far and away the most impressive thing about Nostradamus is that his main tome, *The Prophecies*, has not really been out of print since he wrote it in 1555, which is getting on for 500 years. He may or may not have been the world's greatest prophet, but it's quite possible that his work has made the world's greatest profit.

8. H20 dear (or possibly eau dear)

Arnold Bennett was an English novelist writing at the beginning of the 20th century. He's famous for works such as the *Clayhanger* trilogy and *The Old Wives' Tale*, as well as for an omelette made of smoked haddock, parmesan cheese and cream which was a favourite of his and is now known as the Arnold Bennett Omelette, arguably his greatest contribution to the world.

On a visit to France in 1931 he became embroiled in some consternation about the safety of the drinking water. Arnie was very much of the opinion that all was well with the eau, so much so that he predicted he would be absolutely fine if he drank some of the local stuff. Egged on, no doubt, to put his money where his mouth was, or in this case the water where his mouth was, he duly downed a glass.

At last someone who was prepared to stand by their prediction, someone with the courage of their convictions, a person leading by example. Yes indeed, and for that Arnie deserves some credit, it's just such a shame that his prediction turned out to be so catastrophically wrong. The water was not quite as safe as he had predicted. In fact it was contaminated and shortly afterwards he contracted typhoid and died.

Ah well, you can't make a prediction without breaking a few eggs. Or dying.

9. On top of the world

James Warburg was an American banker who, for a short period in the 1930s, was President Roosevelt's financial advisor. In the 1950s though, obviously much older and wiser, he found himself speaking to the United States Committee on Foreign Relations and uttering this little gemlette.

> We shall have world government, whether or not we like it. The question is only whether world government will be achieved by consent or by conquest.

Well, that's not really the only question now is it? One of the many others is, what the hell were you thinking James? It's quite possible that by making that prediction he single-handedly started the whole conspiracy theory movement and set in motion more paranoia than a ward full of paranoid schizophrenics who were, in fact, being watched and slowly poisoned.

Loons from every corner of the globe, who ironically would do much better if they formed themselves into an organised world movement, probably latched on to what he said and, before you knew it, were harping on about the New World Order, Bilderberg conferences, the moon landings, Princess Diana, the Twin Towers and Paul McCartney, who apparently died in 1966.

As for the actual prediction, pedants might argue that the second part of it is somewhat repetitive and redundant as by saying we'll have world government *'whether or not we like it'*, James is effectively saying what he goes on to say, which is, *'it will be by consent or by conquest'*. Still, if you're going to be completely wrong you might as well be wrong twice eh?

Brilliantly though, it turns out that James had a bit of a past and in 1929 he wrote the lyrics to the hit song, 'Can't We Be

Friends?' which, according to conspiracy theorists, when played backwards clearly says, 'I am a complete arse'.

10. It'll all be over by Christmas

When World War One broke out on 4 August 1914 there were many who rushed to reassure the public that after a quick spat it would all be done and dusted in about five short months allowing them to sit down on Christmas Day to a lovely turkey with the family in a world at peace.

Well, that classic example of stupidly optimistic war time propaganda turned out to be stupidly optimistic, though some people could have avoided total humiliation by claiming that they didn't in fact mean the Christmas coming and were actually talking about the following Christmas. Or the one four years later in 1918.

Nonetheless, despite being proved incorrect time and time again this prediction has been trotted out with alarming regularity on both sides of the conflict in both world wars, which must have been very annoying for the populace; though in the great scheme of things, an irritation such as that probably didn't rank too highly on their list of worries at the time.

One specific example came in 1944 when, talking about an operation codenamed Market Garden, Field Marshall Montgomery said,

Market Garden will be so successful it'll be over by Christmas.

Sadly, the operation to capture strategic positions on the River Meuse and the River Rhine in Holland and Germany was not successful and resulted in the region of 17,000 allied fatalities.

That should really have been the end for the Yuletide prediction, but as recently as September 2009 the Confederation of British Industry (CBI) predicted that the UK's recession would, altogether now, be over by Christmas. It wasn't.

As predictions go it really is foolhardy in the extreme, though incredibly every year there is one group of businessmen and women who persist in trotting it out when making reference to their product; though to be fair to turkey farmers they do tend to get it right.

11. Wake me up when it's Spring and other assorted oddities

In 1967 Herman Kahn and Anthony Weiner released a book entitled, *The Year 2000: A Framework For Speculation on the Next Thirty Three Years*, which contained a section entitled 'One hundred technical innovations very likely in the last third of the twentieth century'. To back up their predictions they stated very clearly that,

> A responsible opinion can be found to argue great likelihood that the innovation will be achieved before the year 2000 – usually long before.

The stage was set then for a truly great fall and, boy, they really didn't disappoint. Thrust forward first was less of a prediction and more of a wish really when they claimed that by the end of the 20th century we would have found,

> physically non-harmful methods of over-indulging.

Oh how the readers must have been desperate for that to come true. No doubt there were many who stockpiled mountains of food, drink and drugs just waiting for the green light on that one, a green light, let's not forget, that they were told would in all likelihood, happen long before the end of the century.

Sadly we're still waiting for that glorious day, but when it comes the world is going to throw the biggest party there has ever been and gorge itself senseless. Then it's going to wake up the next morning feeling absolutely fine. Yeah, right.

Up next was another curio that had many howling. Come the end of the century there will be,

Artificial moons and other methods for illuminating large areas at night.

Ah, that must be one of the same artificial moons used in those artificial moon landings. It does seem odd though. Much as it might be aesthetically quite pleasing to have an artificial moon, why not light large areas with a, erm, light. As for the '*other methods*', it's not clear what they meant though some have speculated that they could be artificial suns, the real sun brought much closer and gigantic, but real, torches.

Finally we come to the prediction voted the worst of all by a panel of experts which states that by the turn of the century we will see,

Human hibernation for relatively extensive periods (months to years).

Narcoleptics everywhere must have rejoiced while everyone else was probably left wondering many things. Why, when we seem to operate perfectly adequately on between six to eight hours a night are they suggesting that we take to our beds for a period of some months or even years? Perhaps deep down they knew that their other prediction about over-indulging was wrong and this was what the world would need to do to sleep off its almighty hangover.

Would we all hibernate together at the same time or would we take it in turns? In which case everyone who was awake would have to tiptoe around really quietly so as not to disturb the sleeping millions. Who would be taking care of the planet while we're all having our extended kip?

The answers may lie in the fact that Herman Kahn was in fact a nuclear strategist and, allegedly, one of the inspirations for Peter Sellers' character Dr Strangelove. Perhaps he thought that nuclear war was imminent and that the only way the survivors could actually survive was by hibernating for years until the radiation levels had come back down. Perhaps. It's more likely that after making all those predictions he was probably a bit tired and fancied a lie down, for three years.

12. Day of give it a rest

What could be better than lazing in bed on a Sunday morning followed by a gentle stroll to the shops to buy a paper and some breakfast or brunch comestibles? Frankly not much, but back in the 19th century American Christian pioneer Ellen G. White was predicting that the 'strolling to the shops and purchasing comestibles' part of the equation would soon be a thing of the past. Ellen had visions and in one of these she foresaw the following.

> The dignitaries of church and state will unite to bribe, persuade,
> or compel all classes to honor the Sunday.

Like William Miller before her (see The End of the World, pp. 220–1) Ellen was very much from the 'if at first you don't succeed, try, try again' school of prediction and reiterated her prophecy on a number of occasions – 1851, 1884, 1888, 1911, take your pick – but what stands out is the fact that she foresaw bribery as a means to this particular end.

That's quite a long-term bribe because presumably she didn't mean that shopkeepers should stay closed for just one Sunday, but every Sunday for the rest of their lives, thus curtailing their earnings till retirement by a whopping one seventh. That would presumably take a considerable amount of cash and no doubt if given the option between persuasion, being compelled or bribery most people would surely plump for the latter.

It's strange though that she predicted those three options

when surely it would have been enough just to compel people to honour the Sunday. Once you're compelled to do something, you have to do it, such as pay tax for example. There's no option to accept a bribe from the state in order to do so.

It's confusing to say the least, but not any more so than the rest of the prediction.

> The lack of divine authority will be supplied by oppressive enactments. Political corruption is destroying love of justice and regard for truth; and even in free America, rulers and legislators, in order to secure public favor, will yield to the popular demand for a law enforcing Sunday observance. Liberty of conscience, which has cost so great a sacrifice, will no longer be respected. In the soon-coming conflict we shall see exemplified the prophet's words: 'The dragon was wroth with the woman, and went to make war with the remnant of her seed, which keep the commandments of God, and have the testimony of Jesus Christ.'

You were warned, though astoundingly Ellen is reported as being, *'the most translated non-fiction author in the history of literature'*. That's a hell of a lot of translators she must have bribed.

13. Idiots ahoy!

Thanks to pictures of this planet taken from space we have a pretty good idea of how many land masses occupy our little corner of the universe, so it's unlikely that anyone is going to find a previously undiscovered new country any time soon.

Nonetheless, new species of animal and plants pop up fairly regularly, and from time to time, a new tribe of some indigenous people or other stick their heads through the jungle foliage, so it's pretty safe to say that we haven't discovered everything there is to discover just yet.

That's not exactly what they thought back in 15th-century

Spain though. In 1486 a Spanish Royal Commission received a proposal from an explorer to set sail west and see what might be out there. In their wisdom they chose to reject it for the following reason:

> So many centuries after the Creation, it is unlikely that anyone could find hitherto unknown lands of any value.

It's a bold prediction, it's just such a shame that the explorer in question happened to be Christopher Columbus. No doubt he took great delight in proving them terribly wrong a few years later when he saddled up the *Santa Maria* and set off on the first of his voyages that did, incredibly, find hitherto unknown lands, some of which actually did have a modicum of value and had already been discovered by someone else or lived in by indigenous people for a bloody long time before he turned up and poked his nose in where it didn't belong.

14. I see a tall, dark handsome prison guard

First things first with this one; technically it is an accurate prediction, but it could so easily have been hopeless and there is something so wonderfully hopeless about it anyway that it's well worthy of inclusion.

Down in Western Siberia they're not averse to popping over to the fortune teller's house and having their palms read, no doubt it helps while away the time during those long winter nights. One man who did just that in 2010 was, reportedly, told by the palm reader that his future involved a *'public house'*, which in them thar parts can apparently be interpreted as a prison and not The Dog and Duck down Omsk High Street. Essentially, he was told that he was going to be doing a bit of porridge in the future.

Obviously the thing to do now would be to keep your nose clean and steer well clear of anything that might seem in the slightest bit dodgy, which is exactly what this fella decided not to do. Instead, incensed by the prediction he tried to kill the fortune teller, apparently hitting her with a knife and attempting to cut her throat. Thankfully she managed to escape and survived, which is more than can be said for the two other onlookers he attacked who died from multiple stab wounds. He's now looking at 20 to life in one of Siberia's deeply unpleasant gulag type nicks where it's predicted he'll be trying extremely hard not to drop his bar of soap in the shower.

As for the fortune teller, well, you might have thought she'd be doing a roaring trade what with her prediction being spot on. Sadly that's not the case, with most people of the opinion that if she's that good, how come she didn't foresee the fact that the guy was going to try and slice her head off. It would have saved them both an awful lot of bother.

15. If at first you don't succeed, Trithemius, Trithemius, shut up

Back in 1482 Johannes Trithemius was heading home from Uni in Heidleberg, Germany, when he got caught in a snowstorm and took refuge in a Benedictine abbey. Whatever they did to him within the walls of the abbey was clearly to his liking because he stayed and the following year was made Abbot no less.

Possibly out of guilt for having given up on his university education, Abbot Johannes set about transforming the abbey into a centre of learning. During his time there its library grew in size, mainly, it would seem, due to his own prolific writings. Old Johannes churned out a fair few tomes, one of which was called *De Laude Scriptorum* or, *In Praise of Scribes*. It's a cracking read with the basic premise being that ... spoiler alert! spoiler alert! ... it's much better to write books by hand.

Printed books, he contends. 'Will never be the equivalent of handwritten codices, especially since printed books are often deficient in spelling and appearance.'

Well, they're only deficient in spelling if they're written by people who can't spell, which applies equally to handwritten books, and they're only deficient in appearance if they're designed by people with the design ability of a warthog, which also applies equally to handwritten texts.

If the spelling and appearance of printed books isn't enough to see them consigned to the rubbish bin though, Johannes comes up with another reason for their demise.

The printed book is made of paper and, like paper, will quickly disappear. But the scribe working with parchment ensures lasting remembrance for himself and for his text.

The printed book is indeed made of paper, but given that the world's oldest printed book bears the date AD 868 and was discovered, in a completely undisappeared form, in a cave in 1907, Johannes really does need to qualify what he means by '*quickly*'.

But the most damning and ridiculous aspect of this whole tawdry affair is that to get his book widely read, Johannes had it printed. On paper! It's like sending an email to loads of people predicting that emails will never replace letters. Or before that sending out loads of letters about how sending messages by letter will never replace an oral message delivered by a messenger on horseback. Or before that sending a messenger out on horseback to tell people that sending a messenger out on horseback to give people messages will never replace smoke signals.

It's bonkers, though it's said that Johannes realised his error and wrote a follow up book entitled, 'Excusum De Abottum Estes Pillockus' or 'Sorry I Got It Wrong, I'm A Pillock, Here's What I Should Have Said', but unfortunately he wrote it on paper and it subsequently disappeared after 37 minutes. No great loss though, as apparently it was full of spelling mistakes and looked shit.

CONCLUSION

So what have we learnt on our travels through the seemingly bottomless pit of predictions that turned out to be so very wrong? Well, for people who are frightened of public reactions to their pronouncements, one thing is pretty clear; unless you have unshakeable, factual reasons for making your prediction, keep your mouth shut.

If, despite this concern, you *do* feel compelled to roll out a prediction or two, make sure you have some sort of emotional or physical insurance policy, like, possessing no shame, or a secret hideaway, in case they fail to materialise.

Many of those who gingerly (or aggressively) stand at the lectern and make their pronouncements do so because they want to shape a brighter future for all of us – with safer streets, cleaner energy, and fast food that doesn't repeat on you. Respect to these souls.

As we've noted elsewhere in the book, predictions do have a very important role to play in society and they can inform planning and design in highly beneficial ways (if they turn out to be right of course). And as scientific advance motors on, futurology is becoming a more developed discipline – with more enhanced and accurate predictive tools. Ridicule some of these modern people and gadgets at your peril. When scientists initially suggested that one day we'd be able to read our own genome map and see whether or not we'd get Alzheimer's in the future, others scoffed mercilessly at them. But those cynics have been proved wrong. In the not too distant future we may well be able to foresee the exact date of our own deaths. Pre-sales of coffins will go through the roof.

But unfortunately there are quite a few predictors whose motivation is not as pure as those who seek to mould a better world.

If you are working on a prototype of a frying pan that doubles as an automated child minder, you might well be tempted to hide behind some very impressive sounding academic qualifications and predict to the world that the frying pan/child minder combo will be available to everyone in the next 18 months. Your hope is that people will get excited and marvel at this brilliant new gizmo and wait with baited breath for it to hit the shops and when it does, purchase it immediately and recommend it to all of their friends. It's a marketing scam – pure and simple.

Another posse of cynical predictors are not motivated by bundles of cash; they're interested in *power*. If you want to build up a cult following, predict with great fanfare that the world's natural life is shortly coming to an end. The more dramatic your prediction the larger and more passionate your following will grow. But make sure you have plenty of prepared statements for your followers when the world doesn't roll off its axis next Thursday as you have warned. ('It didn't happen because you are all so loyal to me'; 'it didn't happen because I bought a special magic kit and stopped it' etc.)

Other predictors are simply inspired by their take on life, making overly optimistic or negative pronouncements that dovetail to their world view. Viewing exactly the same evidence, these two camps can predict blatantly different trajectories.

And what of the way we react to predictions? One can dismiss every prediction as invalid. But that would be foolish. Our responses are often not based on any factual reasoning. Some people poo poo all forecasts because they're scared of change. They don't want their world to be messed with. Even if getting up on Monday mornings is a complete pain in the arse, they'd prefer to carry on doing it, rather than getting up on a new day called Zarsday that contains eleven hours and two breakfasts. They want to keep the status quo – they're happy to be rocking all over the world; they just don't want to rock the world.

The other thing to remember is that on many levels WE KNOW ABSOLUTELY NOTHING. If highly experienced weather forecasters can miss approaching hurricanes and top-flight sports teams lose to very lowly opponents, then what chance have we of making predictions regarding the finer points of the cosmos's development?

In conclusion, let's just imagine for a sultry moment that every single prediction anyone ever makes comes true. We would know with forensic certainty the future that is mapped out for us; what we'll eat at Christmas ten years hence, what kind of shampoo will grow back our lost hair, and whether or not we'll need a windcheater for the summer of 2037.

That would be amazing for planning purposes and diary synchronisation, but it would also be incredibly dull. Part of the joy of life is *not knowing* what's going to happen. It allows us to hope that our tiny lives might gain an increment of satisfaction or wealth. In short, the unknown is knowingly reassuring.

So after spending the entire book slagging off all of those predictors who missed the mark, we salute them for their bravado and for making the future a far more exciting place than it will ever turn out to be.

Long may they continue to be wrong.